Serial CEO:

Lessons From The Climb

T. PAUL THOMAS

I S B N 9798227831842

Dedication

To Jill

My wife, partner, best friend, and my greatest supporter.
You have walked every step of this journey with me.

Author's Note

Early in my CEO career, I had a challenging period with a founder who was threatening to crash the organization into the ground if they didn't get their way. Once everything settled down, one of my board members joked, "Don't worry Paul, someday you will write a book about this and laugh." I guess that was the first time the idea of chronicling my CEO journey came up.

Fast-forward to 2015, when I started writing a monthly column titled "Ask the CEO" for the Flagstaff Business News. For nearly four years, I answered questions and wrote about the various lessons of my CEO journey. One of the readers suggested that instead of the monthly column, I should write a book.

Those two events, along with the realization that there wasn't any single book that existed when I first became a CEO in the mid-90s, have led me to write this book.

While everything you will read is from my 30-plus years as a President, CEO, or Chairman in more than a dozen organizations around the globe, none of this would have happened if it was not for my mentors and friends who helped me along the way. It is these individuals who showed me the way, guided me, encouraged me, and helped me get back up when I fell.

My career and this book are thanks to Jim Buckley, Stuart Chapman, Ross Cooley, Mike Downey, Dave Engelthaler, Tony Ibarguen, John Johnston, Michael T Jones, Will Keiper, Gary Liebl, Frank Lopilato, Bob Mattson, Jeff McKeever, Marsha Morgan, Leticia Palafox, Jeff Sanders and Craig Van Slyke.

And finally, without the support of my parents, Ted and Peg, and my family, Jill, Kayci, Matthew, and Ross, the journey would have never started.

Regardless of where you are in your career, I hope you take away a handful of ideas and lessons that will help you and your career. I hope that you, too, get to experience what I have experienced and that this book helps in some small way to make the journey more enjoyable and fulfilling.

About the Author

T. Paul Thomas is currently an Assistant Professor of Practice and Executive in Residence at Northern Arizona University (NAU) WA Franke College of Business, where he teaches Management, International Business, and Entrepreneurship. In addition, he serves as Director of the Northern Arizona Center for Nonprofit Entrepreneurship, which he co-founded in 2016. Outside of NAU, Paul serves as the CEO of the Northern Arizona Leadership Alliance (NALA).

Before joining the faculty at Northern Arizona University in 2013, Paul was a serial CEO and President, successfully leading more than a dozen publicly traded, venture-backed, and technology start-ups. He led organizations in Africa, China, Europe, India, Japan, and throughout the United States. With over 30 years of being a CEO and President, Paul has experienced nearly everything a leader can experience, and he continues to rely on those experiences as he mentors. He helps numerous organizations and boards that he is a part of today.

Paul has an undergraduate degree in Business Administration, with an emphasis in Finance, and a master's degree in Education Leadership, both from Northern Arizona University.

He currently lives in Flagstaff, Arizona, with his wife, Jill of 40 years, and their dog, Riley.

Contents

Chapter One
Introduction: The Power Of A Mentor

"Great mentors inspire action. Dreaming big is only the beginning. Dreams without action drain vitality and affirm helplessness."

— Peter Drucker

The world loves painting entrepreneurs as overnight sensations, conjuring images of million-dollar ideas and instant success. But in reality, the story is far grittier, more like finding your way through a maze than cruising down a straight highway. Turns are unexpected, detours abound, and uncertainty lurks around every corner. Yet, within this labyrinth of challenges lies the extraordinary: the chance to build empires from scratch and leave your own mark on the world.

This book isn't a magic formula for success. It's a hard-earned map, marked with the victories and scars I've accumulated as a CEO for over 30 years. It's proof that experience, even the challenging kind, is an influential teacher in the leadership game.

Like any journey, whether it is for personal or professional development, it is very important to have an experienced guide, in other words, a mentor. Regardless of your career experience, you may sometimes feel overwhelmed finding your career path in the corporate industry.

In my case, mentorship was the perfect way to work on my professional skills, learn invaluable lessons, and advance my career from someone with years of practical knowledge in my field.

Looking back now, I realize I had early mentors in unexpected places. The scoutmaster of my Boy Scout troop instilled in me a passion for the outdoors and the value of teamwork. Even the manager at the McDonald's I worked at in high school taught me valuable lessons about responsibility and resilience.

Along the way, we'll meet my mentors who light the path, conquer boardroom battles, and discover the quiet moments where authentic leadership shines. This isn't just my story; it's an invitation to design your own entrepreneurial career.

You must be wondering how I started my journey or met my mentors.

Well, my journey began in the hills of West Virginia, where I was born into a family of five children. While material wealth wasn't much, the warmth of family and the lessons learned in those early years became the bedrock upon which my future pursuits were built.

My awareness of economic disparity first surfaced during my college days while visiting my fraternity brothers' homes over a Thanksgiving break. Witnessing the contradictory reality of spacious bedrooms and private bathrooms in my friend's or fraternity brother's family home was shocking. It was through broader interactions that the truth dawned: we weren't affluent; we were simply living with less.

Unlike others who enjoyed individual sanctuaries, our family shared three bedrooms, with my brother and I occupying a single bed. Our bathroom, while functional, offered a bathtub but lacked the luxury of a shower.

Yet, within this atmosphere of scarcity, an unexpected gift blossomed: resilience. The absence of a material safety net fostered a liberating sense of freedom. I understood that the ground beneath me wouldn't disappear even if I stumbled.

This awareness, paradoxically, empowered me to embrace challenges and pursue opportunities with a boldness born from the knowledge that even the most daring venture could never truly diminish what I already possessed: nothing.

My entrepreneurial adventure commenced at a critical crossroads in my established career. After carving a niche for myself in distribution marketing for Compaq Computer and Apple in California, I faced a new turning point. This pivotal moment arrived as a call from William Keiper, an early mentor of mine and previous manager from my early days at MicroAge, who was now the CEO of Artisoft, a publicly traded company in Tucson, Arizona.

Will presented an enticing proposition: to lead Artisoft's marketing department. While the offer held its appeal, my aspirations yearned for greater heights. I candidly conveyed to Will that my ambitions lay in leadership and that a departure from Apple would only be warranted for a president's seat.

With Windows 95's ascent and Artisoft's descent in lockstep, the Board, under Chairman Gary Liebl, found themselves facing the abyss. Their search for someone with new ideas and an objective viewpoint was challenging. My name, though far from renowned in the area of turnarounds, found its way into the mix thanks to Will's persistent advocacy.

With characteristic directness, Gary outlined the stark reality: This presents a pinnacle of opportunity. Resuscitate this company, and you'll not only land on the cover of Business Week but also secure your future. However, failure will shield you with the excuse of joining a sinking ship too late."

The challenge was immense, yet the potential for transformative success was undeniable. Accepting the mantle of President, I was acutely aware of the colossal responsibility and the precarious footing beneath me. Six weeks into my tenure, the Board convened to review my proposed strategies for navigating Artisoft out of turbulent waters.

That evening, Gary's call brought surprising news: the board had unanimously promoted me to the position of CEO. While a personal victory, this promotion bore a bittersweet undertone; it marked the beginning of a ten-year rift with my mentor and friend, Will.

The following years at Artisoft were a blur of high stakes and immense rewards. Under my leadership, the company transformed remarkably from a struggling $2.50 stock to a thriving $ 23-a-share powerhouse.

As Gary had foretold, I achieved financial independence, freeing me to choose future endeavors without the pressure of immediate financial concerns. However, the unpredictable nature of the market was starkly revealed on the day my resignation became public:

Artisoft's stock plummeted 25%, a sharp reminder of the fragility of success and the delicate balance in high-stakes business.

Following my success at Artisoft, my reputation as a turnaround specialist and team builder caught the attention of Silicon Valley's premier executive recruiter, John Thompson. In 1999, he called, beckoning me toward TurboLinux, a company on the cusp of a rollercoaster ride unlike any I had experienced before.

My mission at TurboLinux was twofold: to manage the complex dynamics of the co-founding couple and ultimately guide the company toward an Initial Public Offering (IPO). However, the honeymoon phase was tragically brief. Within two months, the founders tried to orchestrate a coup to remove me from the picture. Fortunately, the wisdom of Gary Liebl from Artisoft proved invaluable, bolstering my position on the board and allowing me to weather the storm.

While working on my exit from Artisoft, I shared with Gary that one of the founders had, at the last minute, requested they keep the CEO title until we completed the IPO. He alerted me to the red flag and said I needed to ask the board, "Who can fire who?" Gary sensed a power struggle would quickly surface and advised me not to accept the job in the event the board didn't agree that I would be able to fire the founders.

During the late-90s 'dot-com' frenzy, TurboLinux transformed into a vortex of venture capital. Every major firm on Sand Hill Road and tech giant eager to exploit the boom overburdened us with investments exceeding $75 million.

Our vision was ambitious: a $15 billion market capitalization despite a meager $10 million in revenue and hemorrhaging cash due to excessive spending. Expensive office furniture, full-page Wall Street Journal ads, penguin-clad mascots parachuting at Comdex, and an international office network became symbols of an unbridled optimism-fueled era.

However, the inevitable dot-com bubble burst, shattering our grandiose aspirations. The company that had captivated investor imaginations faced the brutal sting of market correction. Ultimately, TurboLinux was acquired by a Chinese entity for a fraction of the capital we had secured.

My fruitful relationship and mentor with August Capital, the lead investor in TurboLinux, led me to Intrinsic Graphics (IG), a fledgling company with technical prowess and untapped potential. John Thompson, once again recognizing my aptitude for tackling complex situations, facilitated my introduction to the company. Founded by four brilliant graphics engineers from Silicon Graphics, IG boasted a deep well of expertise in tackling advanced graphics solutions, including those required by satellites.

At the helm stood Michael T. Jones, a man of exceptional intellect, having bypassed traditional education to join Bell Labs as a teenager. My encounter with Michael began a profound professional and personal bond.

Michael chose an unorthodox approach for the final interview, inviting my wife, Jill, and me to share a meal with him and his wife, June. This unconventional step later revealed as a test of my character and suitability for leadership beyond the technical domain, demonstrated his belief that effective leadership extends beyond professional competence.

Upon joining IG, Michael gracefully transitioned to the role of Chief Technology Officer, becoming a trusted confidante and collaborator.

My focus on operational matters complemented his visionary technical prowess, creating a symbiotic relationship that laid the foundation for IG's future success.

As we stepped into the startup world, we secured over $10 million in initial venture funding and embarked on a $25 million Series B round.

However, our trajectory took a tragic turn with the horrific attacks on the World Trade Center. As Michael and I embarked on a trip to London to finalize a critical investment, the tragedy disrupted our plans, leaving us stranded for a week due to the worldwide grounding of flights.

The aftermath of the September 11th attacks cast a long shadow, triggering an unexpected economic domino effect that ultimately led to the retraction of investor commitments to Intrinsic Graphics. Though it was a difficult decision, we eventually opted to sell the company. Still, a fortunate series of events occurred during this closure.

Before the sale, at the urging of our investors, we had spun off a division focused on a promising satellite imagery technology. The spinout was called Keyhole, while the product Keyhole marketed was called Earthviewer. This technology resonated deeply with its potential to democratize access to geospatial information, and it eventually attracted Google's attention. With a significant portion of the IG team transitioning to Keyhole, the seeds of a revolutionary innovation were sown.

Under Google's stewardship, Keyhole's potential blossomed spectacularly, culminating in the Google Earth we know today. Michael, recognizing the profound impact of this technology on global understanding and connection, assumed the role of Chief

Technology Advocate at Google, actively championing the company's positive contributions across the globe. Michael's continued presence on my various boards further solidified our enduring partnership and his mentorship.

By this point in my professional journey, I had established myself as a seasoned captain, adept at navigating the choppy seas of diverse challenges. Throughout my professional tenure, I have had the privilege of experiencing a diverse range of career milestones, including the exhilaration of overseeing Initial Public Offerings (IPOs), and mergers and acquisitions, the challenging task of restructuring corporate entities, and the crucial responsibility of securing funding for business growth. My extensive experience in these areas has positioned me as a trusted advisor for venture capital firms, where I am frequently consulted to assess the viability of companies and, in some cases, provide guidance to steer struggling ventures back on course. As a result, my career naturally evolved towards the role of a serial CEO, occasionally taking on contract or part-time engagements.

Peter Drucker's insightful quote at the start of this chapter brings to light the transformative influence my mentors had on my entrepreneurial journey. They didn't just inspire me to dream big but provided practical guidance on turning my aspirations into tangible achievements. My mentors didn't simply encourage me to shoot for the stars; they showed me how to break down my goals into actionable steps and measure my progress.

William Keiper saw a spark in me even before I did, offering me the marketing role that launched my career. With his unwavering faith, Gary Liebl challenged me to scale the mountain of leadership, pushing me beyond comfort to make real moves at Artisoft. John Thompson recognized my ability to weather storms and placed me at the helm of tumultuous ventures like TurboLinux and Intrinsic Graphics, giving me the platform to prove my mettle. And Michael T. Jones, with his unconventional ways, not only tested my leadership mettle but also gifted me invaluable insights that propelled me forward.

Each mentor, in their own distinct manner, encapsulated the spirit of Drucker's teachings. Rather than simply espousing lofty ideals, they provided practical guidance, offering me the resources, encouragement, and obstacles necessary to grow into a leader who was not afraid to roll up their sleeves and get to work.

The pursuit of knowledge and personal development is rarely a solitary endeavor. Throughout our careers, we encounter individuals who, through their wisdom and guidance, act as catalysts for our growth. These mentors, though not always formally appointed, play a crucial role in shaping our professional trajectories. However, the true value of mentorship lies not only in finding these guiding figures but also in recognizing the need to evolve alongside them.

Just as our professional landscapes shift and our aspirations evolve, so too must our mentorships adapt. A mentor who provides invaluable insights during our early career may not possess the expertise or perspective needed to navigate the challenges of later stages. It is in this dynamic process of change that we find the seeds of further growth. Embracing the need for new mentors, be it through formal programs or informal encounters, allows us to tap into fresh perspectives and expand our knowledge base.

Furthermore, the notion of mentorship should not be confined by rigid formalities. The most impactful guidance often arises from unexpected sources. A seasoned colleague, a passionate entrepreneur, or even a perceptive customer can all assume the role of mentor, offering invaluable insights and challenges that propel us forward. By remaining open to learning from diverse sources, we broaden our understanding and enrich our professional journeys.

Ultimately, the pursuit of mentorship is a lifelong journey, free from age constraints. Whether we are embarking on our first career steps or navigating the complexities of seasoned leadership, the willingness to learn from others remains a cornerstone of success. By embracing the dynamic nature of mentorship, we unlock a continuous stream of growth and self-discovery, ensuring that our professional paths remain vibrant and ever-evolving.

⌒∾

Chapter Two
Building Your Dream Team

"Great things in business are never done by one person; they're done by a team of people."

— Steve Jobs

In the first chapter, the significance of a mentor's presence in your career in order to assist you in personal success and guidance was discussed. When it comes to building a successful organization, the need for a mentor is replaced by the need for teams. There are two key teams required for any organization to succeed: the board of directors (or advisory board) and the management team. Let me touch on both.

The Board Of Directors

From my experience, any CEO or president should set up a board of directors from day one. Others may wonder about the timing, as they might argue that it is too early in the organization's life (no revenue yet, no product, no customers) or that the board will hinder them or even fire them, as you see in the movies. However, rest assured that the correct board can change your life from a struggle through mud to an exhilarating climb.

I've seen it all: receiving an established board, carefully assembling a dream team, and dealing with the ins and outs in between. Every experience was a furnace of tests and priceless knowledge. Finally, we are going to break the code on how one should create a board that will eventually serve as the driving force behind your organization's epic journey.

Step One: Look beyond resumes. Look for people who really want to see you personally succeed. They'll tell it like it is, unafraid of the hard-hitting facts but demanding in their loyalty. Consider your mentors in these situations. With the exception of board members in my publicly traded companies, I persuaded board members to come along for the ride and not for a paycheck. If compensation was the motivating factor, they were not the correct fit. Of course, expenses paid and stock options are a plus.

Step Two: Your board members should be defined by a demonstrably successful career and, preferably, financial independence. Look for those who have achieved personal and, in some circumstances, professional success, which shows they look at contribution, not self-promotion. Those with ulterior motives or a need for approval are less likely to be the rockstar board members you want on the team. I once had a board member who scribbled all through the board meetings, seemingly unaware. However, when he did speak, it was a diamond-cut statement that transformed the entire discourse. He talked very little, but when he did speak, it was solid gold.

Step Three: Compose a board with supporting and offsetting skillsets across key areas such as technology, sales, marketing, legal/HR, operations, and finance. This diversity encourages a broader perspective and helps to guard against blind spots. While the number of members on a board of directors can range widely, my personal preference is a team of five to seven members, promoting a dynamic team environment where expertise is within easy reach without the risk of 'decision by committee.' I've watched boardroom respect grow whenever someone says, "It is an accounting problem; let's hear from our in-house CPA." Having an odd number of members also guarantees you never have a tie when voting.

Step Four: Respect and value your board members. Thinking of them as an "inconvenience" or "necessary evil" reduces their effectiveness and undermines your own leadership. Regular meetings, updates, and appreciation all communicate value and foster a partnership.

I once asked a fellow CEO early in my first CEO role about the board's duties and how I should work with them. He answered, 'Bring them in, feed them, update them, and get them out as fast you can.' Well, that's a disaster waiting to happen. If your board is nothing more than an unpleasant inevitability, something to be tolerated through gritted teeth, you either inherited the wrong crew or took a poor route. More importantly, you are wasting a valuable resource.

Creating a strong board is one thing; making the most of your time together is quite another. Therefore, I have discovered that the following are essential procedures for productive and worthwhile board meetings:

1. Weekly updates: Stay connected with your board through weekly updates. These short reports should update them on the mundane day-to-day things, including HR, sales, and cash flow. They can now

come to board meetings ready to debate strategic issues instead of just sharing basic information.

2. Comprehensive Board Books: The board should receive a comprehensive board book at least one week before each meeting. It should include all agenda items, relevant reports, financials, or other information necessary for an informed discussion and decision-making. By being prepared, your board members will not have to rush to grasp the specifics when they arrive, allowing them to concentrate on making strategic contributions.

In so doing, you pay respect to your board's time and expertise, which, in other words, helps create a joint and productive meeting environment. An informed board is an engaged board, and successful organizations are built on engaged boards.

Your Leadership Team

The journey to organizational success demands two crucial teams: first, as has been explained above, is the board of directors, and the second is the leadership team. Despite having managed the complexities of both inherited and selected or hired teams, I would argue that inheriting the leadership team has several very unique challenges that require patience, action, and brutal honesty.

I spent my first week as CEO holding one-on-one meetings with each team member. FUD (fear, uncertainty, and doubt) tends to be at the top of the mind. They questioned their future and how they fit into the vision. I once had an engineering director come up to me and ask, "I asked around about you, and I heard you always replace your management team. When am I going to be replaced?"

Well, I always have two essential approaches in these situations, which are honesty and openness. In these sessions, I peel off the layers. I talk about their satisfaction, their thoughts on the CEO change (and whether they wanted the job), their evaluation of the company and the current direction, and whether they want to stay and be a part of the team. While also specifying my expectations, I provide a clean exit with severance if someone is not on board. We separate respectfully. No hard feelings, just clarity.

There are numerous benefits to being a serial CEO. After years of hiring, firing, and managing members of the leadership team, you start to learn how to sense who fits and who doesn't. My philosophy? Don't rush. It takes the first 30-45 days to listen to the team, employees, and customers. If they are not in line or a good fit, let them go. This crucible shows who remains and who leaves.

Fortunately, I have identified some of the best leaders in finance, HR, marketing, engineering, and sales. I had the names and numbers of these former executives on the speed dial.

One of those MVPs was Leticia Palafox, who was my CFO/Controller and HR director at five different companies. Personally, this was one of the most important members of the leadership team. Remember that the person responsible for your associates and your cash is so critical. I discovered Leticia early on, and each time a new CEO opportunity opened up for me in the San Francisco Bay area, she would be my first call.

Assembling your Leadership team is a marathon and not a sprint. Be honest, transparent, and decisive. Listen, assess, and act. With the perfect leadership team, your firm will overcome any obstacle and aim at the stars.

Leading Your Team

While external factors like market fluctuations and economic shifts can certainly impact an organization's success, a CEO's most potent weapon lies within team-building skills and leadership. This is more than a bunch of brilliant individuals; it's about creating a team that works towards common goals, effective communication, and unwavering trust. Let's look into the key factors within a CEO's control that can make or break this critical process:

1. Transparency and Open Communication:

- Brutal Honesty from the Start: The one-on-one meetings with each of the team members set this tone. Directly discuss challenges, expectations, and your vision. Instead of avoiding difficult conversations, tackle concerns head-on and create an environment that values open communication.

- Weekly Updates Keep Everyone Informed: Start each week with a leadership team meeting. It doesn't need to be long, and it is designed to keep everyone on the team informed. Keep the team updated on a weekly basis regarding essential metrics, progress, and bottlenecks. This creates a sense of ownership and involvement, meaning everyone is pulling in one direction.

- Weekly One-on-One Meetings with Each Member of the Leadership Team: This is a simple way to stay connected and informed with each member of your leadership team. Schedule an hour each week or every other week if you have a large team.

2. Identifying and Cultivating Talent:

- Know When to Let Go: Do not hold onto inherited members of the team out of loyalty. If somebody isn't right or simply doesn't share your vision, have a clear and respectful discussion. The release opens the way for superior talent and an effective team.

- Listen to the Team, the Employees, and the Customers: The first month is very important for intelligence gathering. Be vigilant concerning employee comments, customer feedback, and teamwork. This valuable input allows you to identify your strengths and weaknesses, as well as potential areas for improvement.

- Your Network is Your Goldmine: Use your prior experience to reach out to a list of former executive contacts. Having a trusted talent pool on hand to fill gaps can be a game-changer.

3. Building Trust and Shared Purpose:

- Lead by Example: Actions do speak louder than words. Be the incarnation of your firm's principles, displaying honesty, diligence, and undivided loyalty to the team's objectives.

- Empower and Delegate: Micromanagement is a formula for failure. Agree on clear expectations, responsibilities, and job requirements. Trust your team members to take ownership of their roles, allocate clearly, and provide them with the necessary resources and support.

- Celebrate Successes and Learn from Failures: The big and small victories should be celebrated. Commemorate victories collectively, encouraging a spirit of unity and a common cause. When you face obstacles, learn from them by analyzing mistakes and changing strategies for future victories. Celebrate publicly and reprimand privately. As the CEO, take 100% of the blame for failures and give 100% of the credit to others for successes.

If, as a CEO, you focus on these key factors, you can transform your team from a group of individuals into an effective team that produces extraordinary results. Keep in mind that your Board of Directors and your Leadership Teams are your strongest tools. Invest in developing them, cultivating them, and managing them with vision, faith, and steadfast determination. The gains will be invaluable in driving your organization to the future of sustainable success.

Role of Teams in the Five Pillars of Success

They say success breeds wisdom. So, would you believe that riding the business roller coaster has endowed me with a wealth of knowledge? And when someone asks me about the secret behind my entrepreneurial journey, I point to five crucial ingredients:

- Mentors: The best mentors are like veteran Sherpas, guiding you through the perilous terrain of business. I've been very lucky to have had people like that in my life. They provided brutal honesty, priceless advice, and a guiding hand when the way became dangerous. Recall that a real mentor is not a cheerleader but a mirror of your true potential and imperfections.

- Board of Directors: It is strange, but some of the best lessons are learned from unexpected teachers. I have been blessed with both great boards and those that could use a little work. The kind of moments that made my vision what it was and filled me with burning desire. I still remember sharing cigars with my board after a Boston Red Sox victory, brainstorming bold strategies, and celebrating shared triumphs.

However, I have met boards where hostility grew, agendas collided, and knives appeared under the shining table. I once had a board member threaten to blacklist me after my resignation, saying he would make sure I never worked again in Silicon Valley. Every painful encounter sharpened my ability to bounce back and learn the ins and outs of power relations.

- Leadership Teams: Just as board members, leaders appear in all shades. My loyal CFO and HR director, Leticia Palafox, shines as an exemplary figure. Her unflinching support, pragmatic guidance, and relentless devotion were a rock in the roughest of waters. However, I've also met young, inexperienced, and ambitious managers willing to give up progress for a short moment of power. Well, this taught me the value of clear expectations and teaming.

Based on such conflicting situations, I have learned the skill of distinguishing between real leaders. This is not about titles or advanced degrees but character, quality, and the ability to influence rather than frighten.

- Hard Work: We all know that there is no shortcut to success. It is a dogged determination, an around-the-clock devotion that consumes all of your strength and passion. My family is a living witness to numerous 'vacations' spent on endless conference calls and early departures caused by unexpected emergencies. The CEO crown bears continuous vigilance, the company's face and champion.

So, yes, accept the long hours and be ready to work harder than everyone else. Remember, the elevator to success only goes up for those who climb the stairs.

- Luck: Occasionally, the fickle mistress of fate throws a curve. Being at the right place and moment, grabbing fleeting opportunities, or avoiding near misses—all these contribute to the complex way of success and failure. I heard someone once say, 'The harder you work, the luckier you get.' While that is true in a way, there is an equally undeniable chance factor that boosts or throws down progress.

But here's the thing: although you cannot manage luck, you can handle your reaction to it. By concentrating on the first four pillars – mentors, board of directors, leadership team, and hard work, you create a solid base that can withstand any trial and bounce back from any adversity. Therefore, accept the risk, keep working, and bear in mind that true success is not the result of a roll of a dice but rather by stick-to-itiveness.

The Secret Of Organizational Success

The real power of organizational success lies outside the boardroom in the unified and high-caliber leadership team. Their harmony, loyalty, and devotion affect the company's course. Everything begins with culture, and the CEO is responsible for setting the tone.

Team Dynamics:

Bear in mind that a winning leadership team is not a group of seasoned individuals; it's a team effort. Respect, open communication, and collaborative decisions make it work in the long run. Early in my career, I worked for a CEO governed by fear and terror. Under his outbursts, his team was afraid to the extent that they were lacking in confidence and initiative. It was a sobering reality of the devastating force of a toxic culture.

Loyalty and dedication power the organization. Building trust with your team, creating a feeling of belonging, and allowing them to own their work is imperative. I was lucky to have a core leadership group that stood by me through thick and thin. My CFO/Controller and HR director, Leticia Palafox, was a constant rock who steered through financial choppy waters and ensured employee welfare with an unflinching focus.

Leading by Example:

As CEO, you define the organizational culture. What you do is more important than what you say. In addition to the regular leadership meeting, I included a weekly one-on-one with each team member. Titles did not determine these sessions; they were safe zones for candid reviews, mutual tribulations, and cooperative resolutions.

My leadership philosophy is simple: They should respect the team, and they should also respect their employees. I learned this the hard way at an early stage when observing how a CEO turned his team against him with his toxic behavior. I swore that I would never make such a mistake again. Never in my 25 years as a serial CEO has anyone on my team heard me raise my voice, swear, or throw anything.

Key Players:

The CFO and head of HR are not merely cogs in the machine but vital components of the organization. The CFO, acting as a conductor, brings financial order to the company, holding the cash flow constant in times of economic upheaval. A reliable CFO by your side is priceless. With her sharp financial skills and unwavering support, Leticia was my partner in the multitude of acquisitions and strategic decisions.

On the other end is the HR head, who is the heart of the team, takes care of the employees, and creates an environment that helps boost productivity. Employee engagement has always been on my list, as I have always been aware that satisfied employees are more productive and loyal to their organization. With people-first, we create a team that feels valued and hence strives for excellence in their work.

Collaborative Effort:

After all, you are not a one-person army. Successful leadership is based on collaboration. The CFO, as well as the HR head, should be your sounding board and not just a yes-person. I've been lucky enough to work with seasoned executives in marketing, sales, and engineering - all parts that bring priceless aspects of expertise. We pushed against one another, sparred back and forth with ideas, and, in the end, built solutions far stronger than any one of us could have developed alone.

Another aspect of collaborative leadership is establishing a good network of executives who are proven performers and can join your team as and when needed. This is the collaborating part from the point of view of employees or people that you work with, forging together seamlessly as and when desired, melding into the existing teams, and contributing towards making you a success.

Expectations and Accountability:

A solid leadership team can be realized through clear expectations and shared accountability. In our one-on-one sessions, the vision for the company was well laid out, as was the role of each individual in the subsequent achievement process. Open communication and regular feedback loops were prevalent so that everybody knew what was expected and worked towards driving the results.

Holding the team accountable did not mean micromanagement but rather promoted ownership and responsibility. Missed deadlines, unfulfilled promises, and unethical behavior were dealt with speedily and transparently. This won the team's trust and created an excellent culture.

Building a Legacy:

Remember, great leadership teams are not just an extension of the CEO; they have their own rhythm and melody. And by setting up a cultural legacy with shared collaboration, trust, and accountability, you build a team that will outlive your tenure. This legacy built from shared values and purpose can continue taking the organization forward long after you have passed on the baton.

In a nutshell, building a successful leadership team is not merely picking out the right personnel; it is all about creating the right environment for them to thrive. That means you will set the cultural tone, collaborate effectively, and hold everyone accountable, which is a way of success throughout every corridor.

Remember: What makes a good board member also makes a great team member. Recruit leaders who share your vision, value your team, and are committed to the public good. With the right players and the right tune, your teams will be transformed into a completely successful organization.

⌒∽

Chapter Three
Red Flags And Wise Decisions

"Your instincts will help you recognize any red flags. Don't let your logic win in such situations."

— Mitta Xinindlu

In this journey, it is important to be aware that red flags always exist. You just need to know how to spot them or listen to others who see what you fail to recognize as red flags. Moreover, wise decisions entail readiness to test, fail, improve ideas, trust in decision-making, high-risk threshold, planning for pivots, and grit and commitment required for success. Considering these factors plus situational analysis, you can make well-informed choices at the onset of your career.

Let me tell you my struggle or blind spot for seeing red flags; as I have mentioned before, I was born in West Virginia. By the time I started elementary school, my family had moved to Ohio. During our time in

Ohio, we lived in a rented farmhouse on a sizeable corn farm for the majority of our stay.

At sixteen, I managed to earn my Eagle Scout award after many years of service as a Boy Scout, which started as a Cub Scout at a very young age. By providing this information about me, I can easily explain that it helped me shape my perspective about how I looked at the world and the people I met.

It is worth mentioning that the Midwest farmers are renowned for their hardworking spirit and steadfastness. Therefore, what you see is mostly a true representation of who they are. So, the Boy Scout Law, which I regard as a life-long guide, prioritizes traits like trustworthiness, kindness, and friendliness, as well as having a sound moral direction. Through adherence to these values, people can develop a strong character and integrity, which are the cornerstones of one's personal development and prosperity.

When my career was starting, I thought everyone seemed to have valid opinions, and I didn't have to worry too much about hidden agendas or red flags. My background as a Midwesterner and Boy Scout was really helpful in addressing challenges that are presented on a day-to-day basis in this real-life situation. To my relief, there were mentors in the vicinity who went out of their way to point out the red flags that I may have easily missed owing to my inexperience.

Early in my career, one of the first red flags that was raised was with my first management position. I was recently named general manager of a division of a public company. I had a team of fewer than 50 employees, including five direct reports. Before commencing the role, I diligently studied numerous management books to prepare for the responsibilities ahead.

Less than six months into my tenure, a group of employees under one of my direct reports approached me with concerning information. They disclosed that their manager was frequently taking extended lunches and returning to the workplace under the influence of alcohol or drugs, or both. Despite having a positive rapport with this individual, I opted to escalate the issue by contacting the Vice President of Human Resources at the parent company.

The Vice President of Human Resources underscored the gravity of the situation, emphasizing the seriousness of the issue that I had initially failed to recognize. She cautioned me that, irrespective of my relationship with the employee in question, it was imperative to exercise caution and handle the matter diligently.

The three of us convened to communicate to the employee the necessity for him to return home and deliberate on two options: either to tender his resignation or to agree to undergo treatment. She made it clear that he was not to return to the office the next day but rather call me with his decision. The whole meeting was characterized by very high emotions—anger, emotional distress, remorse, more anger, and denial. Following the turbulent meeting, it was reiterated that he must contact me in the morning and that he was prohibited from returning to the office.

Following the departure of the employee, the HR executive expressed concern that the individual might attempt to return to the office the following morning and could potentially display violent behavior. Consequently, she advised the presence of a plainclothes police officer in the parking lot as a precautionary measure. This was yet another red flag that eluded my attention.

Arriving at the office at approximately 7:30 am the next day, I presented a photo of the employee to the police officer and firmly communicated that under no circumstances was the individual to be allowed entry into the building. Despite my belief that the employee would not show up, given our good relationship during my time as his manager, my conviction was soon tested.

Shortly after 8:00 am, the receptionist informed me that the police officer was preventing the employee from entering the building. Upon arriving in the lobby, I intervened and assured the police officer that the situation was under control. Addressing the employee, I reminded him of our agreement that he should contact me with his decision and emphasized that he was not permitted to enter the office premises.

I observed the employee's gesture and complied with his request to converse in his truck. As I situated myself in the passenger seat, I noticed a sizable pistol placed on the seat between us, a clear indication of a potentially perilous situation. Despite my relatively brief career at that point, I promptly recognized this as a significant red flag.

Inquiring about the presence of the gun, the employee disclosed his intention to commit suicide and expressed the need to provide an explanation before departing. This was a challenge that no management book could have prepared me for as a person less than six months into a management role.

Drawing on my upbringing on a Midwest farm, years of Scouting, my mom insisting we go to church every Sunday, or my guardian angel, I managed to remain composed. Without panicking, raising my voice, or attempting to seize the gun, I engaged the employee in conversation, encouraging him to express his thinking and needs and assuring him of my willingness to help. Fortunately, the situation concluded without any harm, and the employee returned to work following treatment.

I learned the importance of seeking help in identifying red flags and, more significantly, remaining composed and attentively listening to the individual. Here, he didn't really want to commit suicide, nor was he concerned about his job; he just needed somebody to talk to.

As my career developed and I had more CEO opportunities, being on guard for red flags and listening to my instincts played a central role. This chapter covers one of the main themes—alertness and intuition in the process of making key decisions.

- Recognizing Red Flags: The first step in the journey of decision-making involves the astute recognition of red flags. These subtle indicators, often overlooked in the fervor of new opportunities, serve as cautionary beacons. Embracing vigilance means paying heed to these signals and delving deeper into the nuances of each choice.

As I approach my mid-60s, I realize that with age, our wisdom grows, but we can still be blind to red flags. I often find myself seeking input from my board, mentors, and friends to ensure I'm not overlooking anything. It seems that as we age and gain wisdom, we understand the importance of seeking help.

Recently, a young entrepreneur sought my advice. In his early 20s, he exuded positivity and had ambitious plans. When I inquired about his board, he confidently stated that he was smarter than anyone he knew and didn't need a board. I cautioned him that he might not be aware of what he didn't know and the red flags he might be missing. He insisted that he knew what to do and never needed any help despite me advising him otherwise.

It is important to consult with someone else irrespective of the experience, age, or knowledge that one has regarding a particular topic.

Early in my career, my mentor, Gary Leibel, pointed out a glaring red flag that would have affected my decision to accept a new CEO position. I explained to Gary that the founder was starting to question if he should retain the CEO title until I had been onboard for a period of time. Gary cautioned me on accepting the job until I verified with the board of directors who could fire who. He said if the board doesn't tell you, they will back you up on any decision, including firing a founder don't accept the job. It proved to be great advice when the founder tried to have me terminated after a short period.

That being said, don't allow the potential Red Flags to cause you to get analysis paralysis. Intel Founder and CEO Andy Grove wrote a book titled, "Only the Paranoid Survive." I've seen leaders use that as an excuse not to make timely decisions or take risks.

- Trust Your Gut: Intuition, this acute, inborn sense of knowing, has deep mechanisms of our decisions. Trusting one's instinct, though often difficult in the face of tempting prospects, can lead to pivotal breakthroughs. Intuition guides into careers, and the change is brought into life upon listening to the voice within.

Where signs are not evident, it is necessary to have the capability to consult with others, but I truly believe that most important decisions have to be made through a person's own judgment. In my experience, a bad decision is so often better than no decision at all. For one, a bad decision can be adjusted or even pivoted; indecision can lead to stagnation.

This is particularly evident in situations involving employee termination. You know in your gut that it has to be done, yet you start the "what ifs, the what about, and the what wills." Despite initial doubts and hesitations, I have never regretted terminating an employee in my career.

Managers often cite the excuse that an employee is "just too important right now" as the primary reason for not terminating them. The same goes for the excuse of being "too busy," which is frequently used to avoid taking action. However, if it becomes evident that an employee is no longer the right fit for the role or has been outgrown by their responsibilities, the individual's perceived importance or the busyness of the organization should not serve as an excuse for avoiding necessary action.

Managers should refrain from using such excuses as a shield for avoiding critical management decisions. In almost all cases, managers regret not taking action sooner rather than feeling they acted prematurely. Managers need to recognize that the issues they perceive in an underperforming employee are likely evident to the rest of the team as well.

As CEOs, one of our most demanding and often challenging responsibilities is decision-making. We are constantly expected to make decisions on various matters, ranging from office allocations to long-term strategic plans. It is important to acknowledge that there will always be red flags that escape our notice, hence the need to seek assistance.

However, it is essential not to let the presence of red flags paralyze us. Trusting our instincts, our team and our experience is paramount in making informed decisions. Additionally, being open to pivoting or making swift corrections when necessary is crucial in navigating the complexities of leadership.

Amidst the labyrinth of challenging decisions, the support and guidance of the leadership team and/or board serve as a linchpin in steering a course of action.

- Collaborative Wisdom: Seeking support from the leadership team brings forth a reservoir of collective wisdom and experience. The transformative potential grows from the collaborative insights and the diverse perspectives that emerge from engaging with the leadership team.

- Informed Decision-Making: Leveraging the counsel of the board offers a panoramic view, extending beyond individual perspectives. The role of the board in informing tough decisions is explored, emphasizing the profound impact of their support in shaping pivotal choices.

In essence, the interplay of vigilance, intuition, and leadership and/or board support forms the cornerstone of sound decision-making. Embracing these elements fosters a framework for navigating the complex terrain of career choices, leading to transformative outcomes and enduring impact.

In chapter two, I emphasized the significance of two key teams: the board of directors and the leadership team. When facing a challenging decision, seeking help and advice from these groups is crucial, but the approach is paramount.

In a scenario where things are deteriorating, approaching the board or the team with a statement like, "Wow, things are getting bad; tell me what to do" is not conducive to your effectiveness as a CEO. My approach has always been to follow these steps in such situations:

- Maintain composure and avoid emotional reactions. The board and the leadership team are relying on you to navigate the situation, and they expect to see you in control and maintaining a professional demeanor.

- Gather only the relevant facts without embellishment. It's crucial to demonstrate professionalism and control by presenting the situation with accuracy and precision without resorting to exaggeration or artistic license.

- Present the options you have identified, along with their respective pros and cons. Maintain a factual and unbiased approach, ensuring that the information provided does not distort anyone's perception or opinion.

- Clearly articulate the option you are inclined to pursue, including the timing, expected outcomes, and the rationale behind your decision.

- Encourage candid feedback, advice, and the identification of any potential red flags that may have been overlooked.

The quote, "*Your instincts will help you recognize any red flags. Don't let your logic win in such situations.*" serves as a reminder to prioritize gut feelings when facing red flags, even if they may seem counterintuitive at first. By combining vigilance, intuition, and collaborative wisdom, we can make sound decisions that lead to fulfilling and impactful careers.

Chapter Four
Managing People: The Art Of Leadership

A key to achieving success is to assemble a strong
and stable management team."

— Vivek Wadhwa

Managing people requires more than just looking over tasks and delegating responsibilities. It requires a good knowledge of human dynamics, excellent communication skills, and the ability to inspire and lead people toward common goals. This is one of the major challenges in managing people: assembling a team that is not only competent but also cohesive and aligned with the organization's vision and values.

Vivek Wadhwa's quote emphasizes that effective and stable management is a must and one of the leading success factors. This highlights the importance of leadership in establishing organizational balance. A strong management team sets the tone for the entire workforce, providing direction, guidance, and support to drive performance and foster a culture of excellence.

However, building such a team is no bed of roses, and it needs sound selection and nurturing of talent, backed by effective leadership development programs that groom the new generation of leaders well in advance. Further, maintaining stability within the management team, especially against changing market dynamics, evolving business strategies, and personnel changes, is really a very difficult task.

Another challenge in managing people is interpersonal dynamics and conflict management within the team. Effective communication, resolving conflicts, and emotional intelligence lead to a work environment that is collaborative and supportive, making individuals develop and contribute best at their levels.
It implies that when managing people in the modern-day work environment, human resource management has a huge element of diversity, fairness, and inclusion. Diversity, inclusivity, and equity present a higher power to an organization's ability to innovate and respond while strengthening the environment of belonging and respect.

Now that I am currently teaching at Northern Arizona University, I have so many students who are curious about how I reached this level of CEO. I will always try to pass on the information that while individual work and efforts account for a large percentage of success, in the real sense, our achievements are molded through the support and help that we receive from other people along the way of our careers. These "other" people could be our mentors, the management team, our family, and mostly the associates we work with within our organization.

They also often ask what kind of books they should read, what their GPA should be, what to wear, how many hours of work they need to be given, or even which classes they need to take. While these may have aspects of their own, I personally find that the credit for founding the basis of success goes to having outstanding mentors, managers, and employees right from day one of my career.

In this chapter, my aim is to emphasize two crucial points for you to take away. Firstly, it is vital to recognize that success is not solely about individual abilities or innate talents. It is about acknowledging and appreciating the invaluable support and guidance received from others. Secondly, expressing gratitude to those who have played a pivotal role in our professional growth is of utmost importance.

It's Not About You, Your IQ, Or Your Genes.

Success is not purely based on an individual's personal characteristics, for example, having a high IQ or the genes that one is born with. The truth about success is that it emanates because of intelligence, dedication, learning from failures, and growth. It all plays a bigger part in achieving the goal and developing to fulfill one's potential.

Extraordinary achievers like Elon Musk, Bill Gates, and Warren Buffet epitomize the inviolate truth that success hardly ever blooms in a vacuum. Along the way of this journey called life, driven and brought by the combination of ambition and the ability to set tough targets for themselves, people are influenced by support from other parties and action in such a deep way to determine a course and further acting like a driving force toward realization.

Who knows? This guidance and chance to grow in life could come from parents, early career mentors, or even a manager at our first job.

As our professional paths progress, we often rightfully attribute our achievements to the invaluable guidance of mentors, leaders, and colleagues we encounter along the way. However, I posit that the contributions of our team members and the employees within our organizations stand as a particularly significant and often under-recognized factor in our individual successes.

I highlight through this book the influence of only a few who have had a major influence on my journey. It is only fair to say, though, that, indeed, the list would be long, and the people contributing to making me successful have been many. Yet, I have always tried to stay very conscious of the fact that these very accomplishments, from the first job I ever had to my position today, are all the fruits of someone taking a risk on me, giving me an opportunity, or speaking on my behalf. It is an understanding of the contribution and risks borne by others on our behalf that might be the best evidence of our gratitude and humbleness. It offers a very strong reminder of the nature of the relationships that bind our lives together and necessitates us to nurture them and build supportive environments for each other in a professional context.

Ask Questions, Be Inquisitive, And Seek An Uncomfortable Stomach.

A curious mind and a little discomfort can bring growth at both personal and intellectual levels. Inquiring is to go where no one has gone. It is stepping into uncharted waters. Curiosity and the ability to handle discomfort prospects moving forward and guarantee that one has much more of a large worldview than the size of life currently lived. This is exactly the process that will increase our understanding, creativity, and problem-solving abilities. One of my colleagues once gave everyone a good shake when he suddenly left the job.

When I inquired about the reason behind their decision, they shared an intriguing insight. They explained that they had noticed their stomach no longer felt the familiar discomfort that arises when faced with challenges or pushed outside of one's comfort zone. This realization prompted them to seek new opportunities elsewhere.

As an employee, I would strongly encourage you to embrace discomfort and actively seek out mentors or approach your manager to explore new avenues that stretch your abilities. It is rare for a mentor to proactively seek out a mentee, so taking responsibility for seeking guidance is crucial.

Constantly striving to take on additional responsibilities and actively seeking opportunities beyond your areas of expertise or assigned responsibilities is a hallmark of those who achieve success. Individuals who consistently ask questions, challenge the status quo, and take the time to learn from experienced employees within the organization tend to thrive.

Also, listening is important—spending 80 percent of the time listening and 20 percent speaking—is a rich practice. So many times, we end up talking too much, forgetting the wisdom and insights we may get from listening.

Learn how to be uncomfortable, seek guidance, take on new challenges, and listen actively to be able to personally grow, develop new abilities, and develop an attitude toward new ideas and approaches.

Remember To Thank Those Who Saved You While You Thought You Were Drowning.

The idea of gratitude is the act of giving appreciation and acknowledging the support extended by people in times of need, most especially when a person feels that he or she can manage the complexities of life alone. With the help of others, we mostly sail during rough times. Whether a mentor, a friend, or, more bluntly, a stranger, you have gratitude toward them for the impact they had on your life.

Looking back at my career, I can only be grateful for the opportunity through which I had the chance to interact with and offer service to organizations across the country. There is somehow a worrisome trend whereby some attribute success to internal abilities, with organizations mirroring individuals, and this has just added to the list of pet peeves.

A poignant example involves a start-up CEO who sought my assistance. Despite multiple meetings spanning several months and my uncompensated efforts, the CEO repeatedly expressed a lack of immediate financial resources while offering "founder's stock" as future compensation should the company experience a turnaround.

Two years later, upon the organization's acquisition for a significant sum, I never received any acknowledgment or fulfillment of the promised stock options.

Fortunately, such instances are the exception rather than the rule. The majority of organizations I collaborate with demonstrate a commitment to maintaining relationships and honoring obligations, particularly during periods of financial prosperity. This basically emphasizes the reality that organizational success is rarely based on internal tassels but flourishes on the collective contributions of many individuals. That makes it of utmost importance to instill a sense of appreciation and reflect sincere thanks to all those who actually work to make the organization reach its objectives.

Managing Is Really Tough.

Hence, the broader perspective presents the conclusion that managing and handling any team or organization is a very hard and tough job, where not only handling tact but a lot of skills and abilities are required. It's full of responsibilities and pressures; sometimes, the situation becomes overwhelming. This includes tough decisions to be made, managing conflicts, and making sure everything goes in line with the smooth functioning of the team or organization. Effective management requires in-depth knowledge about various things, like communication, problem-solving, leadership, etc.

The book titled "Management Would Be Easy… If It Weren't For the People" by Patricia J. Addesso captures the common sentiment shared by many managers. The task of managing employees can be incredibly challenging, yet it remains an essential responsibility. Without a dedicated workforce, an organization cannot thrive, resulting in a lack of products, sales, and clients.

As a CEO, the role of managing can be frustrating at times. It can be likened to being a former successful athlete who transitions into coaching a team. Watching them execute, seeing their mistakes, and witnessing when they fail from time to time could cause a very strong temptation to intervene. But one should always remember that, as a CEO, your main task is not to execute everything but rather to motivate, influence, teach, and coach the organization toward success.

When the team or employees you lead achieve victory and success, there is an unparalleled sense of fulfillment. It is important to acknowledge that the triumph is attributed to the collective effort of the team. Without them, you could not achieve success, and that is why their commitment and loyalty should be appreciated and praised.

Have An Open Door And Tough Skin.

Open communication and approachability in the environment establish very effective management. This open-door policy should make employees feel free to express their thoughts, ideas, and concerns at any time. That seems to develop a transparent and collaborative culture inside the organization. Nevertheless, managers should be hardy and unemotional in the face of any challenge or criticism. Toughening the skin would help the managers take something constructive, even from the setbacks and feedback, while keeping the climate around them and their team optimistic and supportive in nature.

In a workplace, therefore, understanding that every employee is different and realizing that what works to motivate one may not necessarily work with another is an important lesson in management. The question then becomes how these differences are identified and the primary motivators of each employee determined.

One thing of importance, and always considered by me, when I start my new job is to meet face-to-face with each associate in the organization. There is a list of questions that I would normally ask in a one-to-one conversation to understand the purpose of the interviewee and the environment the person prefers.

1. Who Are You, And What Do You Do?

Engaging in these individual meetings served multiple purposes. Firstly, it allowed me to ascertain the preferred form of address for each associate, recognizing that not all individuals named Robert may prefer to be called Bob. The conversations further brought out the way the employees actually felt about their positioning in the organization, understanding that they actually belong to the responsible lot at their respective desks and how much it means to them. Some of the answers also stated whether the employees were actually satisfied with the positions they were occupying in their respective careers.

2. How Long Have You Worked Here, And How Many Times Have You Considered Leaving?

Regarding the latter part of the question, my main focus lies in understanding the reasons behind an employee's decision to actively seek alternative employment opportunities. In 95% of cases, employees have been forthcoming and honest during our one-on-one meetings. This level of honesty can be attributed to a combination of factors, such as my relatively new presence within the organization and the assurance of confidentiality that I provide.

If I discover that a significant portion, around 15-20%, of the associates I am acquainted with are actively looking for other opportunities, it serves as a clear indication of a potential problem. This situation raises a red flag that demands immediate attention. Subsequently, I follow up by inquiring about the specific reasons that prompted their consideration to leave or actively pursue interviews elsewhere. If the issues they highlight are related to the organizational culture, management, or other factors within the organization, I offer a proposition. I request a period of 90 days to address and rectify their concerns.

Additionally, I guarantee them that if the problems still linger after this deadline, I will help them secure a more favorable position.

3. If You Were Me, Coming In As The New CEO, What Three Things Would You Change, And What Three Things Would You Leave Alone?

This statement serves as an indirect inquiry regarding your consideration of leaving and the reasons behind it. It reflects the personal perspective of individual associates in identifying areas that require attention and those they are content with.

Conducting an all-employee meeting following the completion of one-on-one discussions is of utmost importance. During this meeting, it is crucial to discuss the feedback received without disclosing the identities of the individuals who provided it. For instance, you may mention that "a significant majority of the team inquired about the possibility of obtaining free parking."

Neglecting to address the feedback shared during an all-employee meeting may convey a lack of attentiveness or a disregard for their time. It is essential to be transparent about what can and cannot be addressed. For instance, I once encountered a situation where our company lacked a paved parking lot, resulting in a muddy mess during rainy weather. I had to be honest with them and let them know that there was no way we could fund the paving at that time.

My door is actually open at any time, both physically and metaphorically, for any associate to come and ask questions, share their thoughts, or discuss anything with me. Starting these first one-on-one meetings allows each associate to get to know me better so they are more comfortable and open to talking with me.

However, it is important to develop thick skin in this role. By actively seeking feedback and requesting honest opinions, one must be prepared to receive both positive and negative feedback. I once led a technology company despite having limited knowledge about the intricacies of the actual technology. I am neither a technologist nor do I claim to be one. During my first all-associates meeting, I encountered a situation where one of the lead engineers stood up and questioned, "Do you even know anything about our product or technology?"

Thick skin is a vital attribute for a CEO, as it is impossible to please everyone. A mentor once advised me that if the goal is to be liked by everyone, then a managerial role may not be suitable. From my experience, it appears that approximately 20% will consider you exceptional, 20% will view you unfavorably, and the remaining 60% will generally be content with your performance. My mentor's guidance was to focus on the middle 60% rather than investing efforts in attempting to win over the bottom 20%.

While the accuracy of these percentage figures is uncertain, I found it crucial to prioritize the overall success of the organization rather than worrying about being universally liked. A CEO must possess a resilient spirit and maintain an open-door policy to tackle the responsibilities of management effectively.

Do Your Employees Stress Their Annual Reviews?

Effective employee management involves conducting annual reviews where managers sit down with their employees to discuss performance and provide feedback. It is crucial for employees to feel comfortable and well-informed during these reviews, which can be achieved through consistent feedback throughout the year.

The greatest focus is on the employees' feeling that an annual review is something routine. The following can be done in this line:

1. Establish Clear Expectations, Goals, And Objectives: Right from the beginning, roles, responsibilities, goals, or objectives to be achieved by the employee need to be defined very clearly. All the expectations at this juncture have to be clear right now so that no form of confusion creeps in in later stages.

2. Provide Regular Feedback: Managers need to ensure that they are giving feedback at every opportunity that arises within the day. While positive feedback may come naturally, it is equally important to address areas for improvement or correct any mistakes. By consistently providing feedback, employees will always be aware of their progress and whether they are meeting expectations and goals. It is detrimental to save issues for the annual review and surprise employees with feedback they were unaware of.

3. "Are You Doing Okay?" When encountering an employee in passing, it is common to ask, "How are you doing?" or "How's it going?" However, a subtle change in phrasing can elicit a more meaningful response. Instead, try asking, "Are you doing okay?" You may be surprised by the difference in the employee's reaction. Just as it is important to avoid surprises during the annual review, it is equally crucial to prevent surprises regarding employee satisfaction or the possibility of them seeking new opportunities. While regular one-on-one meetings with employees are ideal,

casually checking in by asking, "Are you doing ok?" provides an additional means of receiving feedback.

4. Make The Annual Review Two-Way: Prior to conducting a formal annual review, encourage employees to write their own review. Ask them to assess their performance against each objective and goal. However, it is essential to approach this exercise with diligence and not view it as a shortcut to writing the review yourself. As a manager, it is your responsibility to invest time and effort into crafting a thorough and comprehensive review before requesting the employee's input.

5. Be On Time: It is of utmost importance to ensure that annual reviews are delivered on time. Hearing from an employee that their review was due weeks, months, or even quarters ago is something to be avoided. Remember, each of them is an essential employee to any organization—employees who take care of the customers and deliver exceptional products and services through teamwork, proper management, transparency, and accountability in any organization.

6. Praise In Public And Criticize In Private: This should be done on the bedrock principle of praising in public and criticizing in private, which, on the one hand, may come to be applied during your annual reviews and, on the other hand, needs to permeate even continuous feedback. Be sure to set aside some time during the weekly all-employee meetings to publicly give light on outstanding performance, individual achievements, and success by any of the employees, which will go a long way in maintaining a motivated and contented workforce. No monetary awards or prizes necessarily need to be spent; sometimes, a few words

describing the actions that have a positive impact on the organization are enough.

On the other hand, you should avoid criticizing your employees in public. Public criticism works as a serious demotivator and can demolish the morale of your subordinates. Even when discussing inappropriate behavior or the job performance of a subordinate, such talks should not be emotional, dramatic, or exaggerated. Calmly explain to the employee what he did wrong, explain the negative impact it had or could have, and inquire about how you can assist the employee in preventing those same mistakes from happening in the future.

I had a conversation once with an employee responsible for sales. He possessed exceptional knowledge about our products as well as those offered by our competitors. Despite lacking formal sales training, he had a likable personality and a talent for winning people over. However, his sales numbers began to decline, and he started arriving late and leaving early. He told me that he had some private problems, which were part of the reasons he couldn't concentrate and stay motivated. After a number of conversations, I explained that I had to let him go; his performance really just didn't measure up to our expectations.

Two weeks later, he expressed gratitude toward me. He acknowledged that his unhappiness and termination had forced him to confront reality. He made a complete career change, achieved success, and continues to maintain contact with me.

Do You Really Care?: In my perspective, to effectively fulfill the role of a manager within an organization, it is crucial to possess two essential qualities: genuine appreciation for one's employees and a strong sense of empathy. While there may be managers who hold differing opinions or may attempt to prove otherwise, I personally believe that working under someone who lacks sincere appreciation and empathy would be impossible.

As a management professor, the time has often come to tell my students that management is not an academic exercise and a person cannot be an outstanding manager from any book; at the end of the day, it is a matter of an individual really caring about others' success and welfare.

What I usually share with the students is an incident like the one above, in which the employee was feeling troubled by something outside of the organization. For such incidents, the Management 300 textbook had no particular solution. But if a person is empathetic, then he will be in a position to listen and make the employee feel respected before effectively handling the situation.

No doubt, management has large rewards, too, but it also has its own predicaments. In all this, it never has to be lost on the manager that management is not about him but the employees, who are of great significance within the organization.

Chapter Five
Listening As A Leadership Skill

Of all the skills of leadership, listening is the most valuable — and one of the least understood. Most captains of industry listen only sometimes, and they remain ordinary leaders. But a few, the great ones, never stop listening. That's how they get word before anyone else of unseen problems and opportunities."

— Peter Nulty, Fortune Magazine

Although I've transitioned from the corporate world to academia, my experience as a serial CEO continues to shape my perspective. I've consciously strived to avoid adopting the traditional "academic" mindset. Instead, I draw upon my practical experience to bridge the gap between theory and practice. Throughout my career, I've used the terms "leader," "leadership," and "manager" interchangeably, recognizing that these roles often overlap and complement each other.

Management textbooks often portray leaders and managers as distinct entities, rarely coexisting within the same individual. While there's some truth to this notion, the business world offers numerous counter-examples. Walt Disney, for instance, embodied the visionary leader, crafting a compelling vision of the future for his company. Conversely, his brother Roy served as the perfect counterpoint, meticulously managing the financial aspects, procedures, and processes that kept the company running smoothly. In my view, leaders offer direction and inspire their teams to achieve great things, while managers provide the roadmap and tools necessary to navigate the journey toward those goals.

However, the reality for most serial CEOs, myself included, is quite different from the idealized "Walt and Roy" scenario. We don't have the luxury of a dedicated partner to handle the intricacies of management while we focus solely on leadership. Instead, we must be adept at wearing both hats, seamlessly transitioning between leadership and management as situations demand.

This chapter doesn't delve into the debate of "leader vs. manager." Rather, its focus lies on the specific skills, actions, and thought processes that distinguish true leaders from mere managers. While I've touched upon various aspects of leadership throughout this book, the five key elements listed below have been instrumental in my leadership journey.

Five Qualities of a Great Leader

Throughout my career, I've been asked countless times what it takes to become a successful leader. In my experience, exceptional leadership precedes the CEO title; if you cultivate these qualities, success often follows. This chapter outlines five key principles that I believe are fundamental to becoming a great leader:

1. It's Not About You

Early in my career, I had the privilege of working under and learning from Ross Cooley, a phenomenal leader. One evening, while working late, he took me to dinner, constantly interrupted by colleagues and clients wanting to greet him. I jokingly remarked that he must dislike eating out. His response resonated deeply: "They come to see me because I'm the President of Compaq, not because I'm Ross Cooley. Never forget that. It's not about me." He further emphasized that when he ceased to hold that position, the attention would cease as well.

This lesson resonated deeply. Fast forward to 2013, I was seeking advice from Craig Van Slyke, a former academic leader, as I transitioned from the corporate world to academia. He echoed Ross's sentiment: "Remember, it's not about you, it's all about the students. You're moving from the top of the pyramid to the bottom."

These lessons are crucial. If you hold a leadership position and believe it's about you, you need guidance. It's about serving those entrusted to your care.

2. Communicate Openly and Consistently

The importance of open and consistent communication within an organization cannot be overstated. From overarching strategies and business plans to financial results and hiring initiatives, all employees deserve to be informed on a regular basis.

Throughout my career, regardless of the organization's size, I held regular Friday meetings with all employees, providing comprehensive updates and welcoming questions. Honest and open communication is vital; failing to do so allows rumors and misinformation to spread, fostering anxiety and uncertainty. These meetings also presented opportunities to celebrate successes, recognize outstanding contributions, and offer public praise while keeping critiques private.

During a challenging period of financial uncertainty, I provided weekly updates on fundraising efforts, including potential investors, amounts considered, and success probabilities. Additionally, I informed everyone of our projected timeline should fundraising fail. Not a single employee resigned during this period, a testament to the power of transparency.

While open communication fosters trust, it also means facing difficult questions. Once, an employee inquired about potential layoffs. Denying the truth would have shattered trust when the layoffs eventually occurred. Instead, I acknowledged that all expenses were undergoing review, expressing my hope for minimal employee impact.

Finally, admitting "I don't know" is not a sign of weakness. It's far better to acknowledge a lack of knowledge and commit to finding an answer than to offer a false or misleading response.

3. Mom (or Others) Are Watching

As a leader, you represent your organization 24/7, 365 days a year. Your words and actions, regardless of setting or occasion, reflect on the organization as a whole. By conducting yourself with the understanding that someone you respect, such as your mother, children, or spouse, is always observing, you increase the odds of leading effectively.

Early in my career at Apple, I sent an angry email to a colleague. Immediately after hitting "send," a wave of regret washed over me. It felt as though all 14,000 employees had received it. This experience emphasized the power and permanence of emails and social media. Remember, emails are rarely truly deleted, and impulsive responses can have lasting negative consequences.

To further solidify ethical and responsible behavior, imagine every employee observing your actions and decisions. This approach ensures fairness and promotes a culture of respect within the organization.

4. Never Believe You're the Smartest One in the Room

There's a tendency for some leaders to believe they are the wisest individuals in the room, particularly during senior management meetings. This mindset is detrimental to organizational success.

Instead, strive to surround yourself with the most intelligent and capable individuals you can find. Don't be deterred by insecurity or self-doubt; true leaders aim to build organizations that can thrive and flourish even in their absence. Ask yourself: "If I were unavailable for 30 days, how would the organization fare?" Ideally, the answer should be "business as usual," not a celebratory party thrown by relieved employees.

Great leaders empower their teams, encouraging growth, promotion, and opportunities to showcase their talents. They encourage questioning and challenging perspectives, fostering a dynamic and innovative environment.

A respected individual invited me to join his executive team during my career. Initially hesitant, I expressed my concerns about working under someone else. He assured me we would work collaboratively, not in a traditional boss-subordinate dynamic.

However, after months of evaluating potential acquisitions, I presented a recommendation that...included acquiring a competitor to dominate the industry, alongside divesting a struggling company division where we held a minimal market share. The CEO vehemently rejected my proposal, refusing to even consider my reasoning. When I reminded him of our collaborative agreement, he responded, "I'm the ship's captain, and what I say goes." This experience solidified my belief in the importance of listening, even to opposing viewpoints. I resigned shortly thereafter.

Less than a year later, the newly appointed president contacted me, informing me of their decision to sell the very division I had recommended divesting. He acknowledged the validity of my recommendation, highlighting the value of diverse perspectives and the importance of open communication within a leadership team.

This experience underscores the crucial point: a leader's position doesn't guarantee infallibility. Embrace the power of listening, even when faced with disagreement, as it can lead to better decision-making and improved organizational outcomes.

5. Find the Little Things that Matter to Your Employees

Beyond financial compensation, employees seek fulfillment and purpose in their work. As a leader, it's your responsibility to identify what motivates and inspires them. It could be something as simple as offering an occasional early dismissal, providing opportunities for professional development, or simply taking the time to learn about their personal lives and families.

Early in my career, I worked at a technology company under a CEO whose leadership style raised red flags. Upon joining the company, he proudly shared a quote from a business publication regarding his work ethic, stating that he hadn't been home to hold his newborn child in six months. This anecdote served as a stark reminder of the kind of leader I aspired not to be.

Leadership is a privilege, not a right. If you are fortunate enough to hold a leadership position, strive to earn the respect and dedication of your team, not their fear and distrust. By prioritizing transparency, open communication, and the well-being of your employees, you can cultivate a thriving organizational environment where everyone feels valued and empowered to contribute their best.

Remember, exceptional leadership is not about wielding authority or seeking personal gain. It's about fostering trust, inspiring others, and collectively achieving extraordinary outcomes. By embracing these five core principles, you can embark on the rewarding journey of becoming a truly great leader.

Three Requirements For Becoming A Great Leader

Based on my nearly 40 years of experience in business, leading organizations with up to 500 employees, three key requirements stand out for becoming a great leader:

1. The Ability to Listen and Observe:

   - Observe and learn from leaders around you, both good and bad. Pay attention to their behavior in various situations, noting their strengths and weaknesses.

- Example: Witnessing a CEO's anger and unprofessional behavior during stressful times served as a valuable lesson in maintaining composure and treating employees with respect.

2. The Ability to Care and Possess Empathy:

- Demonstrate genuine care for your employees, prioritizing their well-being and success over your own.

- Self-reflection: Honestly assess your motivations for wanting to be a leader. Is it driven by genuine care or personal gain?

3. The Willingness to Admit You Don't Know Everything:

- While possessing foundational knowledge is crucial, acknowledge your limitations and seek help from your team when needed.

- Example: Feeling comfortable saying "I don't know" to questions about technology or visionary aspects and relying on team expertise demonstrates humility and a willingness to learn.

In conclusion, Nulty's quote, emphasizing listening as the "under-appreciated" core of leadership, aligns perfectly with this chapter. Each of the five qualities presented, from leadership to fostering open communication, requires active listening to understand and respond effectively.

This attentive listening extends beyond mere actions to encompass potential consequences, as highlighted by the "Mom (or Others) Are Watching" principle. Similarly, empowering teams and valuing diverse perspectives necessitate actively listening to their ideas and concerns.

Ultimately, Nulty's insight underscores the true essence of leadership: fostering trust, inspiring action, and achieving collective goals through the power of listening. By prioritizing this often-overlooked skill, leaders can cultivate a thriving work environment where everyone feels valued and heard.

$$\backsim$$

Chapter Six
Everything I Needed To Know About Business I Learned From My Newspaper Route

"At an early age, I started my own paper route. Once I saw how you could service people, do a good job, and get paid for it, I just wanted to be the best I could be in whatever I did."

— Sean Combs

Many students inquire about the specific experiences that have shaped my journey toward becoming a CEO. Upon reflection, one of the most valuable business lessons I have ever learned originated from a rather unexpected source: my childhood newspaper route in Ohio. It was there, delivering the Ravenna Record-Courier, that I gained foundational knowledge that has consistently served me throughout my career.

It is unfortunate that opportunities that exist within such a route for a young person are no longer possible.

At the age of eleven, I was responsible for delivering newspapers to my community. This daily routine, encompassing fifty newspapers delivered every day except Sunday, spanned a period of three formative years. Unknown to me at that time, such business fundamentals were sinking into me, which, within a short span, dramatically affected the course of my professional life. The following paragraphs will elaborate further on the specific lessons I drew from being a newspaper delivery boy. These lessons, rooted in the seemingly ordinary act of delivering newspapers, have proven to be universally applicable and continue to guide me in my current role as a CEO.

The Value Of Customer Service

The cornerstone of any successful business lies in understanding and exceeding its customers' expectations. This fundamental principle, though seemingly simple, is often overlooked. My experience as a newspaper delivery boy served as a powerful early lesson in the multifaceted nature of exceptional customer service.

Case Study 1: Delivering The Perfect Newspaper

One of the first and most crucial lessons I learned was understanding individual customer preferences.

While the act of delivering a newspaper may seem straightforward, I quickly discovered that meticulous attention to detail was paramount in fostering customer satisfaction. Initially, I naively believed that simply throwing the newspaper from my bike would suffice. But I quickly found that as soon as the wind decided to blow, the pages inside the paper would lift and sometimes land helter-skelter across the lawns and the driveways, which was an inconvenience to the customer.

From this exercise, I found that most customers would request that I instead get off my bike and walk those extra few steps to drop the paper right at their door, or between their screen door and front door, or in a mail or paper box ensuring it was where they could get to it easily. This little inconvenience left a lot of marks on customer satisfaction. It taught me to go the extra mile in every small task.

The essence of exceptional customer service lies in tailoring your approach to individual needs. While my customers in my Ohio neighborhood shared a similar cultural background, venturing into diverse contexts necessitates a deeper understanding of different preferences and expectations. Unlike my local customers, who readily provided their preferred delivery locations, clients in unfamiliar cultural settings may have implicit expectations that require proactive inquiry and cultural sensitivity.

Case Study 2: Respecting Cultural Differences In Business

This principle was profoundly reinforced during a business dinner in China with the Minister of Aerospace. As the countless dishes arrived at the table, I, exhausted from a long flight, struggled to navigate the cultural nuances of dining etiquette.

Faced with an unfamiliar dish, I hesitantly took a small spoonful and pushed the bowl away. To my surprise, the Minister, speaking impeccable English, gently advised me of the dish's significance and high value in Chinese culture. This experience was a stark reminder of respecting cultural differences and avoiding assumptions.

Engaging in international business means being proactive in approaching cultural knowledge. This will include historical aspects, customs, and etiquette regarding a specific region, thus ensuring that behavior is consistent with local expectations so as not to cause an unintentional offense. Practicing good cultural sensitivity and respect in a place of work can earn one respect and credibility and build a client base from varied cultural backgrounds.

In other words, lessons from those years as a "news bag-bearer" boy are more valuable than I could expect. Knowing your customers, not surprising them, relating to them on an individual level, and respecting cultural differences is critical in customer care for any profession or cultural setting. When you do this in a business setting, you will instill a sense of loyalty in them and ensure that your business relationship with them thrives.

Financial Responsibility

One can compare this by saying that just as a strong foundation is important for a building to stand in all weathers, financial responsibility also forms the foundation of the business so that it may stand strong in all economic tides. Lessons in financial prudence: being a delivery boy for the Daily Paper taught me the pivotal nature of cash flow in determining business health.

Cash flow is the continuous movement of money in and out of a business. It is considered the bloodstream of a business as it forms a lifeline that is instrumental in forming financial tasks and offering a way to operate. On my paper route, I would get a bill from the newspaper company every week based on how many papers I had delivered.

While I collected money from customers each week, the feeling of having a collection bag filled with cash often led to the misconception that I had readily available funds. However, I quickly learned the crucial distinction between having money and having spendable money.

The collected funds were not for personal use but to cover the cost of the newspapers. Only after fulfilling my financial obligations, which included paying the newspaper company, could I consider spending any remaining money on personal items. This experience taught me the importance of prioritizing financial responsibilities before indulging in personal spending.

This principle of responsible financial management translates directly into the business world. Businesses must:

- Pay bills on time: Meeting financial obligations promptly fosters trust with vendors and suppliers, ensuring the smooth flow of goods and services necessary for business operations.

- Budget carefully: Creating a realistic budget helps businesses allocate resources effectively, avoid overspending, and ensure sufficient funds are available to cover essential expenses.

- Avoid overspending: Resisting the temptation to spend beyond available means is crucial for maintaining financial stability and preventing debt accumulation.

- Be prepared for unexpected challenges. Setting up an emergency fund will at least cushion the effect of financial hiccups that may occur occasionally.

How these principles matter is more pronounced when one considers that starting a business is a very risky venture where hardly 25% of businesses survive up to 15 years. Failure in businesses actually depends on a myriad of factors, but financial mismanagement, to a great extent, is among the leading causative agents.

I learned not to spend the money I had collected after selling newspapers before paying for them, and businesses learned to be prudent with their finances to ensure longevity.

Those in the organization who control all the aspects of budgeting directly in their enterprises may better focus on managing economic difficulties toward business development and, in turn, result in success.

The Cornerstone of Reliability

Reliability is a fundamental pillar of any successful business. It encompasses consistently meeting customer expectations and delivering on promises, regardless of external circumstances. This principle, ingrained in me as a newspaper delivery boy, has proven invaluable throughout my career.

Delivering Through Challenges:

While seemingly mundane, the act of delivering newspapers presented its own challenges. The mean Ohio weather, which scorches people during summers and gives chills in winters, will be a test of my commitment. Delivering newspapers on such a bitingly cold and snowy night, particularly at eleven, was not an easy task. But the experience instilled in me the need to keep at it and be faithful to one's responsibilities.

Meeting Customer Expectations:

In the service industry, reliability transcends personal circumstances. Customers expect to receive their products or services consistently, regardless of external factors. They rely on the business's dependability to meet their needs and maintain their trust. Excuses and justifications, however valid, hold little value in the face of unmet expectations.

The Importance of Contingency Plans:

Building and maintaining reliability requires proactive planning and preparation. Recognizing that unforeseen circumstances can arise, it is crucial to establish contingency plans to ensure uninterrupted service delivery. This involves identifying potential challenges, developing alternative solutions, and ensuring the necessary resources are readily available.

This principle manifested in my brother's service as a backup during my newspaper delivery career. When unforeseen circumstances prevented me from completing my deliveries, he seamlessly stepped in, ensuring that customers received their newspapers without disruption. This experience highlighted the importance of having a reliable support system and fostering a culture of collaboration and accountability within an organization.

Ensuring Business Continuity:

The importance of being reliable is considered paramount, especially in the current scenario of the international business environment. International travel for important business meetings or conferences brings a lot of 'ifs'; for example, jet lag, airport congestion, long security lines, and 'what if' kinds of situations. Realizing this, whenever I used to go on an international trip, I would always give buffer days so that in the case of an unexpected travel schedule delay, something over which I had absolutely no control would not ruin a crucial meeting or cause me problems elsewhere.

The experience of delivering newspapers instilled in me the profound importance of reliability in building and maintaining successful business relationships. The ability to consistently meet customer expectations, overcome challenges, and deliver on promises is essential for any organization seeking to build trust and achieve long-term success. By fostering a culture of reliability and implementing strategic contingency plans, businesses can navigate the complexities of the marketplace and ensure consistent service delivery, even in the face of unforeseen circumstances.

Finding Balance: A Journey of Work, Life, and Enjoyment

Life, like a well-written story, requires balance to thrive. This principle applies not only to our personal lives but also to our professional pursuits. My experience as a newspaper delivery boy was an early reminder of the importance of prioritizing different aspects of life while finding joy in the journey.

Balancing Responsibilities:

Quite often, I was tested against one's professional commitment while delivering newspapers. Because many of my friends lived on my newspaper route, opportunities to play kick the can or a quick game of backyard football always came up. But it could be the things that sow the seeds of late deliveries or backfire from unhappy customers.

From that experience, there had to be remuneration—a certain fill-in for the balance. Balancing it in such a way leaves time to carry out a responsibility or achieve a certain level of productivity without affecting well-being or neglecting other meaningful connections.

Prioritizing Family and Self-Care:

Balancing between career, family, and personal well-being is one of the elusive struggles in my career. With this in perspective, I would regard my family as grounds for anything I possess. My work and other responsibilities issue me with priorities, but only second to the welfare of my family.

While your priorities are your organization and your family, don't forget that you need to also take care of yourself. Take the time to do the things that allow you to recharge your batteries, regardless if that means meditation, yoga, working out, or just relaxing over a weekend and reading a book.

Incorporating Enjoyment into Work:

Finding enjoyment in our work, regardless of its nature, can significantly enhance our overall experience. So, the point here is that, just as I used to get off my bike while delivering newspapers, to play with friends from time to time, I feel that it is relevant to find those moments of joy and satisfaction within professionally respective paths.

Whether it is a new challenge, working with new colleagues, or, certainly, marking the testimony of a job well done, such an experience can be a motivator for yielding an enjoyable working life.

Learning from the Journey:

The lessons learned while earning from delivering newspapers as a child proved transcendent through the years, proving their applicability in all walks of life and business. The importance of balance, prioritizing, and, most importantly, not losing sight of the struggle to have fun always forms the guiding light. With this acceptance, it becomes easier to maneuver through life's complexities and build better relationships that fuel success in personal or professional life.

Chapter Seven
Assessing Organization Culture: Day One
Through Employee Resignation

*"Company cultures are like country cultures. Never try to change
one. Try, instead, to work with what you've got."*

— Peter F. Drucker

In this book, we will not debate or argue about the possibility of changing company culture. Instead, we will focus on the importance of assessing the organization's culture and the opportunities to do so while you are the leader. Assessing the organization's culture is crucial in understanding its values, norms, and behaviors. This assessment allows leaders to gain insights into the culture's current state and identify areas for improvement.

As Peter F. Drucker famously observed, company cultures hold a certain resemblance to national cultures. Like the traditions, customs, and languages that define a nation, company cultures are deeply ingrained values, beliefs, and behaviors that influence how employees interact, make decisions, and approach their work. These cultures evolve over time, shaped by the company's founders, leaders, and past experiences. Much like trying to fundamentally change a country's culture overnight, attempting to radically overhaul an established company culture can be daunting and potentially disruptive.

Assessing Company Culture

As a new leader, understanding your organization's culture is crucial. Here are a few methods you can implement to get a feel for the company's atmosphere:

- Individual 1:1 Meetings: Remember those one-on-one meetings discussed in Chapter 4 that you were supposed to have with employees when you first started. Those are a goldmine of cultural insights. If you haven't done them yet, prioritize scheduling individual chats with everyone. Consider group meetings of 3-5 employees for larger companies or tight schedules.

  After these meetings, don't keep the information locked away. Share your findings back with the employees. This shows you value their input and builds trust. Imagine if you poured out your heart about the company's environment, only to have it fall on deaf ears. Transparency builds a foundation for open communication and future cultural assessments.

- Buy your associates lunch their first week and last day: Gathering honest feedback from new hires can be tricky. You've just wrapped up one-on-one meetings with your team, but there's still more to learn about the company culture from a fresh perspective. Taking new employees to lunch during their first week and again on their last day can be a goldmine of information.

Lunchtime with a new hire offers a chance to understand how the company is perceived externally. Ask them why they were interested in the company, how they thought it would be different from their previous job, and where they learned about the organization. This sheds light on the company's reputation and how effective your recruiting efforts are.

Another valuable topic is the interview process. Were they treated professionally? Did they feel respected and appreciated throughout the experience? How long did it take, and could it be improved? Their insights can help you streamline and strengthen your recruiting strategy.

Perhaps most importantly, you can learn about their first-week surprises, both positive and negative. Waiting a few days after they start allows them time to settle in and notice these details. While potentially uncomfortable, the negative surprises are crucial for identifying areas that someone entrenched in the company culture might overlook.

Ending the lunch with an open invitation for them to continue sharing their thoughts, ideas, and concerns lets them know you value their perspective, even after the regular lunches stop. An open-door policy reinforces this message and encourages open communication.

The purpose of the lunch on their last day is entirely different. First and foremost, it's an opportunity to express gratitude for their contributions. Be specific! Mention changes they implemented, improvements they made, and how you personally benefited from their presence on the team.

Now you can delve deeper: why are they leaving? Money is rarely the sole reason, but it's often the easiest answer. Since they're no longer worried about job security, they're more likely to give you honest feedback about their decision to resign.

Resist the urge to counter their new offer or try to convince them to stay. While tempting, it's not a sustainable practice. However, you can ask if anything could have changed their mind or if there was anything you could have done differently to make them want to stay. Prepare for some frank and possibly emotional feedback about their experience. This information is invaluable for improving the work environment and preventing future resignations.

Connecting with new hires during these critical points in their employment journey can provide valuable insights and strengthen the company culture for everyone.

How to handle an associate's resignation?

Resignations can be tough for managers. Our first instinct might be panic – we're already stretched thin, and losing someone adds to the workload. However, resignations can also be a chance to strengthen your company's culture.

Instead of focusing on the immediate inconvenience, try flipping the script. How can you make this a positive experience for the departing employee? It might feel counterintuitive, but remember – good management isn't about you. Treating the resigning employee well sends a message to everyone else on your team. You show that you value them and that their happiness matters.

This positive approach has a ripple effect. The employee who leaves on good terms might become a great brand ambassador, speaking highly of your company to others. They might even be a strong reference for future hires.

Early in my career, I had two very different experiences regarding two resignations that couldn't have been more different. In both cases, I was leaving for fantastic opportunities within the same industry.

- Traditional Negative Approach by Managers

  The first instance happened in 1989. I was working at a computer franchise company called MicroAge. When I told my manager, he requested that I keep it quiet until he had a chance to inform the senior team. A few hours later, we entered his usual staff meeting. He abruptly said, "Before we begin, Paul has resigned and must leave the meeting." That was it. I was excluded from all meetings moving forward. This felt particularly unfair since I'd been named Employee of the Year the previous year. After four years at the company, I felt cast aside and punished for no reason. My colleagues seemed awkward, too.

  Positive Resignation Experience Example

  Four years later, resigning from Compaq Computer was a completely different experience. My manager, Ross Cooley, wanted to maximize my contributions before I left. He included me in every meeting and even arranged a meeting with HR to discuss the new company's recruiting and hiring process. He even threw a going-away party for me!

These experiences were polar opposites. One made me feel valued and appreciated, while the other made me feel like an afterthought. Shouldn't managers care about how resigning employees feel?

- Importance of Positive Resignation Experience

What truly baffles me is when managers or companies treat departing employees poorly. What message does that send to the remaining staff about how they'll be treated if they pursue new opportunities? More importantly, who would want to stay on your team if you're a manager who shuts out resigning employees? The way you handle resignations absolutely impacts your company culture.

I've even witnessed situations where organizations immediately escort resigning employees out the door, forbidding them from ever returning to the office. These were valued, high-performing employees! We all know people don't stay at the same company forever, so why treat them poorly as they advance? Furthermore, how can you expect to attract top talent to fill the vacancy if they hear how the previous person was treated? If the departing employee had a negative experience, why would they speak positively about the company?

Here's the crux of the issue: Why do some managers make resignations a positive experience while others make it miserable? In my opinion, the bad managers take it personally. They see themselves as the center of the organization, and every resignation reflects poorly on them. They might even view it as a vote of no confidence. It's not about you, manager! Stop taking it personally.

Celebrate the new opportunity for the departing employee. See them as a seed you're planting in a new organization. Treat them as an ambassador who will spread positive word about the company they left behind. Consider them a reference for future hires. Imagine what I would have said if someone had contacted me for a reference about working at Compaq Computer or for Ross Cooley!

Management by Walking Around

The simplest, yet perhaps most underutilized, method for assessing company culture is simply walking around and interacting with employees. This is especially important in larger organizations spread across multiple buildings or floors.

Here's how to make the most of this approach: Block out dedicated hours each week on your calendar to walk the halls. It's ideal to have some background knowledge about what each employee is working on, perhaps a recently completed project. Stop by an open door and offer congratulations on a job well done, inquire about their next project, and see if there's any way you can assist.

Remember any issues or concerns raised during individual meetings or initial introductions. As with other situations, ask insightful questions and demonstrate genuine interest in their responses. Strike up conversations about a photo, a desk item, or even a piece of art on the wall. Take notes electronically or on paper to keep track of any commitments you make.

Here's a real-life example: Our College of Business has five floors, with faculty offices on the third and fourth floors. During summer break, most faculty are away except for a handful who are teaching classes or conducting research. Once, a new dean started during the summer and made a point to walk these floors at least twice a week. This was their chance to introduce themselves, hear faculty thoughts on the college, and gain a deeper understanding of the culture. By the fall semester, they had a solid grasp of the culture, a group of faculty who could spread positive words to others, and built rapport with a core group.

A final tip: When practicing "Management by Walking Around," keep things fresh. Don't always start in the same hallway or floor, and avoid visiting the same offices or cubicles repeatedly. Always ask if someone is too busy to chat before engaging them in conversation.

Changing an organization's culture is akin to turning a large cargo ship into a strong current without any power. It's achievable but requires significant time and careful navigation. However, by consistently assessing and understanding the culture, you can take corrective steps and better manage the situation at hand.

$$\backsim$$

Chapter Eight
The Power And Perils Of Email

"There's a temptation in our networked age to think that ideas can be developed by email and iChat. That's crazy. Creativity comes from spontaneous meetings from random discussions. You run into someone, you ask what they're doing, you say 'wow,' and soon you're cooking up all sorts of ideas."

— Steve Jobs

Effective communication has always been the cornerstone of successful business interactions. In the past, businesses relied heavily on face-to-face meetings and written correspondence to convey ideas, negotiate deals, and build relationships. However, the arrival of new technologies has significantly transformed the communication landscape.

The arrival of the telephone definitely ruffled some feathers in the business world back then. People worried that face-to-face interactions, where you could read a person's expressions, were crucial for sealing deals. Today, there's a similar grumbling about email and texting. Some folks argue that these methods are taking away from the "proper" way of conducting business.

I see email and texting as fantastic tools, but just like any tool in the toolbox, they need to be used for the right job. Unfortunately, their ease of use and speed can be a double-edged sword. Because it's so quick to fire off a message, some people rely solely on them, neglecting other communication methods.

While email's history stretches back to 1971, it really exploded in popularity during the mid-90s. By now, after over 30 years, you'd think everyone would be well-versed in email and texting etiquette. But I still come across some head-scratching emails occasionally.

Here's the thing: by following a few simple guidelines, we can ensure we're using the right tool for the right situation and avoid any potential communication pitfalls.

1. Think Twice Before Hitting Send

We've all been there - composing an email in the heat of the moment, letting frustration or anger flow freely onto the keyboard. It might feel good at the moment, but trust me, hitting send on that email is a recipe for disaster. Those messages are best deleted as soon as you finish writing them.

Instead, consider taking a calmer approach. Try sending a quick email to the person you're upset with, simply asking if they have a few minutes to chat and clear the air. There's no substitute for a face-to-face conversation to work through disagreements.

2. Assume a Wider Audience

This is a golden rule for email safety: write with the mindset that everyone in your organization could potentially read what you send. This will naturally make you more cautious about the content of your emails.

Following this rule means avoiding confidential information, personnel issues, or anything personal in nature. You might think this is being overly cautious, but let me tell you from experience, it's not.

In one instance, my IT department purposely set up my email to BCC them on every message I sent. Another time, I sent a company-wide email discussing our financial situation and fundraising efforts. Within hours, a reporter from the local paper called, wanting to discuss the details in my email.

Sure, the reporter could have called me even if I'd delivered the message in person, but having a written email with my signature removes any doubt about its authenticity.

3. Keep it Brief

Here's my personal rule: if your email requires more than a few sentences, it's probably not suitable for email and needs a conversation or meeting. There will always be exceptions, of course, but lengthy emails often get buried in my inbox to be read "later," which often translates to "never."

With the constant barrage of emails – spam, work discussions, personal messages, and updates from your team – it's easy for inboxes to overflow. Be considerate of others, keep your subject line clear, and keep your email concise.

If I do need to send a longer email, I make a point to apologize upfront and summarize the key points in the first few sentences. For example, I used to send a detailed, two-page email to my board members every Friday. To make it easier to digest, I'd include a quick summary at the beginning, highlighting key sections like sales figures, cash flow, and product development updates.

4. The Power of the Pen

This tip might make me sound old-fashioned, but I strongly recommend keeping the art of handwritten notes alive.

I used to take the time to write birthday and work anniversary notes to my employees. It took effort, but you'd be surprised how many of them proudly displayed those notes in their workspaces.

Handwritten notes are especially impactful when expressing gratitude. Sadly, thank-you notes seem to be a dying breed these days. I can't recall the last time I received a physical thank you note from a couple whose wedding I attended.

In the business world, a handwritten note can make you stand out from the crowd. After a job interview, consider sending a quick thank you note expressing your appreciation for your time and reiterating your interest in the position. Most people won't do this; even a simple email will likely be overlooked.

Give it a try for a month! When you want to thank someone, show appreciation, or acknowledge a job well done, swap the email for a handwritten note. You might be surprised at how much a small gesture can mean.

5. Reply Responsibly

One thing that really gets under my skin is the excessive use of "Reply All." In over 30 years of emailing, I can't think of a single instance where it was truly necessary. Maybe when coordinating a department potluck, but that's about it. Take a moment to consider who actually needs to see your reply before hitting "Reply All."

Another pet peeve is the colleague who uses email as a self-preservation tool. They'll send an email, often negative or about something someone didn't do, and copy everyone in the organization. Resist this urge! If you have an issue with someone's work performance, send a quick email requesting a private conversation to discuss it. Even better, offer your help in getting the task completed.

Here's a golden rule I try to follow: use "Blind Copy" (BCC) for large group emails. This prevents the "Reply All" enthusiast from accidentally responding to everyone, and it hides everyone in the group's contact information.

There's one exception to the BCC rule. If you need to contact someone externally and also keep someone within your organization informed, don't use BCC. Instead, forward the email after you send it. For example, I once needed to address a performance issue with an employee in another state, and I wanted HR to be aware of the situation. I mistakenly BCC'd the HR director, who then replied to the email and corrected something I'd written. This alerted the employee to the fact that it was a personnel matter.

6. Beware: Emails Last Forever

This might seem obvious, but it's worth emphasizing: emails never truly disappear. Every email ever sent is likely sitting on someone's computer, an old server, or even a Google data center. Just like assuming everyone in your company can see your emails, remember that no email is ever truly deleted.

If the permanence of emails isn't enough to consider, they can also be forwarded indefinitely. This reinforces the importance of following all the other email etiquette guidelines I've outlined. Think before you send; remember, your emails could potentially follow you forever.

7. Mind Your Tone and Language

When it comes to email communication, tone, punctuation, and emojis are all important factors to consider. Always think about your audience and tailor your message accordingly.

I generally view email as a casual communication method, so my tone reflects that. Of course, there are situations that call for a more professional approach. But for the most part, I focus on ensuring proper grammar and avoiding typos. Thankfully, autocorrect makes it easier than ever to achieve well-written emails.

Think of it like a toolbox: having the right tool makes any project go smoother and delivers better results. The same goes for business communication. Email and text are valuable tools, but they're not the only ones in your arsenal. If you want to achieve optimal results, choose the right tool for the job. Don't rely solely on email for everything.

In conclusion, while email and texting are powerful tools for communication, Steve Jobs' quote reminds us that true creativity thrives on face-to-face interaction. The passage reinforces this concept by highlighting the importance of choosing the right communication tool for the situation.

Just like a toolbox isn't complete with only a hammer, effective business communication requires using a variety of methods, from email for quick updates to in-person meetings for brainstorming sessions. By understanding the strengths and weaknesses of each communication method, we can leverage technology to enhance, not replace, the power of personal interaction.

Chapter Nine
Connecting With Competitors

"There is a tendency among some businesses to criticize and belittle their competitors. This is a bad procedure. Praise them. Learn from them. There are times when you can cooperate with them to their advantage and to yours! Speak well of them, and they will speak well of you. You can't destroy good ideas. Take advantage of them."

— George Matthew Adams, Columnist

In the business world, competition is often viewed as an obstacle to overcome. However, in my experience, a healthy level of competition can be a tremendous asset. Having competitors in the marketplace serves as a valuable form of validation. It confirms a genuine need for the product or service you're offering.

Think about it this way: if you're the only one selling something, it might raise a red flag. Perhaps there's a fundamental reason why no one else has entered that particular market space. On the other hand, competition suggests that you've identified a viable market with growth potential.

However, the benefits of competition extend far beyond market validation. Competitors always push you to come up with new ideas and make things better. Imagine a football team in high school that never plays anyone else. If you don't have to play skilled opponents, there's not much reason to improve your plans, come up with new plays, or train harder. In the same way, competition in business keeps you on your toes. It makes you constantly look at what you're selling, find ways to make it better and aim for excellence.

As CEO, the first 60 to 90 days are all about a few key things: business culture, employee well-being, financial health, and customer happiness. Once I have a good understanding of the company's internal and customer-focused parts, I start to learn about the competition. Studying your competitors can help your business grow.

Understanding Your Competitors

To be successful in business, you need to know everything about your competitors. The first step is to find out who your closest competitors are and where they do business. This may seem like a simple thing to do, but depending on your business, there may be direct competitors who offer similar goods or services and indirect competitors who may meet a similar need for your target audience in a different way.

Once you know your primary competitors, you should learn more about them and what makes them different. What makes their products different from yours? What do you think their skills and weaknesses are?

The good news is that there are many tools that can help with this study. An easy Google search can reveal a lot about your competitors, including their website content, marketing materials, and even customer reviews.

People who used to work for a competitor and now work for your company can also give you useful information. These people often have a unique view because they have seen how your competitor works from the inside. There is a lot you can learn about your competitor's strategies, culture, and possible weak spots by having polite talks with them.

Initiating Communication With Competitors

Establishing a line of communication with your competitors might seem counterintuitive, but in my experience, it can be a powerful strategic move. The key lies in approaching the interaction with a genuine desire for connection and mutual understanding.

Once you've identified your key competitors, consider reaching out to their CEOs directly. A brief and casual email can pave the way for a productive conversation. There's no need for overly formal language or a detailed agenda. Here's an example of what I've used in the past:

Dear Jane,

While we haven't had the pleasure of meeting, I've been following your impressive work at XYZ for the past four years. Coincidentally, I'll be in Dallas for a vendor visit in two weeks and would love to treat you to lunch. There's no hidden agenda – I simply believe connecting with a fellow industry leader would be valuable.

Best regards,

[Your Name]

This approach has proven successful for me over the past three decades. In most cases, CEOs have been receptive to the idea of grabbing lunch. There was only one instance where a CEO declined, questioning my motives. Interestingly, that particular company is no longer in business.

Here are some key things to remember if you decide to initiate contact with a competitor:

- Keep it casual: Remember, the goal here is to build rapport, not pry for confidential information. The CEO has likely done some research and is familiar with your background, thanks to online resources like LinkedIn and your company website.

- Focus on relationship building, not interrogation: This is not an opportunity to grill your competitor about their latest product or delve into their financials. Come prepared with thoughtful questions demonstrating genuine interest in getting to know them and their organization.

- Transparency is key: Be upfront and honest if the CEO asks why you've reached out. Acknowledge that while you may be competitors at times, you believe there's value in building a personal connection. Mention that unforeseen opportunities for collaboration might arise, and you simply want to connect while you're in their city.

Following these suggestions can transform a potentially awkward situation into a positive and productive interaction. Remember, fostering a spirit of collegiality within your industry can lead to unexpected benefits down the road.

The Benefits Of Meeting With Competitors

There are several compelling reasons to cultivate relationships with your competitors through face-to-face meetings. The first and most immediate benefit is establishing a personal connection with someone who understands your industry's unique challenges and opportunities. Having a direct line of communication with a competitor's CEO allows for a more collaborative approach to navigating the marketplace.

This direct access proved invaluable in a situation I once encountered. During a bid for a big project, a competitor's salesperson told some very obvious lies about our business. They lied to the possible client when they said we were in serious financial trouble, which was clearly not true.

I was able to get in touch with the competitor directly because I had already built a relationship with their CEO over a casual lunch. I told them what happened and clarified that I knew sellers sometimes lie, but this was a clear case of outright lying. The CEO truly apologized and promised that they would talk about it with their agent. Thankfully, our honest communication ultimately won us the project.

Building connections with competitors can also open doors to strategic collaborations down the road. In one instance, initial conversations sparked during a lunch meeting eventually led to a successful three-way merger between my company and two competitors. Each organization possessed unique strengths and weaknesses that perfectly complemented the others. While one company ultimately decided not to move forward, my company merged with the remaining competitor. This strategic partnership created a much stronger entity that quickly became a dominant force within the market and continues to thrive today.

The potential benefits extend beyond full-blown mergers and acquisitions. Competitors may sometimes identify underperforming divisions within their own organizations. If they're looking to find a suitable new home for such a division, having a pre-existing relationship can position your company to acquire that asset and integrate it into your own operations.

Finally, there's the unexpected benefit of forging genuine friendships with fellow CEOs. There are times when leading a business can feel lonely. To build a network of peers, you can talk to and share experiences with them, make connections with competitors who face similar problems, and know how stressful it is to work in the same industry. The friendships I've made with some CEOs of competitors over the years still exist today, showing how important these ties can be for support and camaraderie.

Addressing Concerns And Potential Downsides

While I've consistently found these meetings with competitors to be valuable experiences, I understand there might be some concerns. One common worry is the potential for trade secrets to be leaked. Let me assure you, in my extensive experience, this has never been an issue. The focus of these interactions is on building rapport and gaining a general understanding of your competitor's landscape, not exchanging confidential information.

There have been instances where CEOs have asked detailed questions about my company's operations. However, I've always been able to gracefully redirect the conversation or provide high-level information that doesn't compromise sensitive details.

The biggest red flag to look out for might be a competitor who only seems interested in getting information and doesn't seem to want to connect with you. A talk where they dominate the conversation and ask a lot of questions might be a sign that they have something else in mind. In these situations, it's fine to politely leave the talk or steer it back to a more balanced exchange.

In conclusion, fostering positive relationships with competitors can be a surprisingly strategic move. George Matthew Adams's quote perfectly encapsulates this philosophy: *"There is a tendency among some businesses to criticize and belittle their competitors. This is a bad procedure. Praise them. Learn from them. There are times when you can cooperate with them to their advantage and to yours! Speak well of them, and they will speak well of you. You can't destroy good ideas. Take advantage of them."*

Building relationships with competitors' CEOs has helped me in many ways over the course of my work. Not only do these links give you useful information about your competitors, but they can also open up unexpected ways for you to work together, like mergers or acquisitions.

Also, talking directly to the leaders of your competitors can help you solve problems quickly and easily. In the example I gave about the dishonest salesperson, I could talk directly to the competitor's CEO about the problem because I already knew them. This protected our interests and got us the job.

In the end, competition is good for business and helps it grow. It forces you to come up with new ideas, improve, and stay ahead of the game.

By getting to know your competitors on a personal level, you can turn them from enemies into valuable resources. This will make the business world more cooperative and, eventually, more successful.

Chapter Ten
Decisiveness: The CEO's Ultimate Skill

"It turned out that getting fired from Apple was the best thing that could have ever happened to me. The heaviness of being successful was replaced by the lightness of being a beginner again."

— Steve Jobs

Throughout my career, I've come to believe that a crucial skill separating good CEOs from great ones is decisiveness. This isn't just about making quick choices; it's about making them effective. At the same time, the speed of the decision might seem like the harder part; ensuring its effectiveness is the true challenge.

In a previous chapter, I discussed the importance of surrounding yourself with a strong support system – mentors, a capable board, and a talented management team. These individuals play a vital role in evaluating complex decisions and exploring various options. Ultimately, however, the buck stops with the CEO. We are the ones who have to make the final call, and we have to live with the consequences, good or bad.

Here's a personal takeaway I've learned about decision-making: sometimes, a bad decision is better than no decision at all. If a choice turns out to be wrong, there's usually room to adjust course and correct it. It's crucial, in those situations, to take full responsibility for the misstep and explain the steps being taken to rectify it. Transparency and accountability are key leadership qualities.

On the other hand, when a decision yields positive results, the credit should be shared with others: the team, colleagues, the board – anyone who contributed to the success. Remember, effective leadership isn't about self-aggrandizement; it's about guiding a team toward shared goals.

The Toughest Choice: Letting an Employee Go

Looking back on my years as a CEO, one of the most challenging decisions I've faced is when to terminate an employee. While policy violations are clear-cut and necessitate swift action, the situation becomes more complex when it's about someone who simply isn't the right fit anymore.

There are two main reasons why this decision can be so difficult. First, the employee might occupy a critical role within the organization. Letting them go could have unforeseen consequences for both the team and senior leadership. Second, there's the factor of loyalty. Perhaps the employee has been with the company for a long time, demonstrating dedication and commitment.

However, the key factor at play here is whether the individual still aligns with the company's needs and vision. This chapter delves into the challenges and decision-making process involved in letting an employee go when they are no longer a good fit or the position itself has evolved beyond their skillset.

Outgrowing the Role: The Importance of Continuous Growth

Throughout my career, I've come to understand that, just like any decision, hiring an employee isn't a lifelong commitment. Think about it – we don't expect the choices we make to be permanent, and the same applies to our employees. We hire individuals to fill specific roles with the hope that they'll develop and potentially even move up within the organization. However, realistically, if an employee remains stagnant in the same position with the same responsibilities for several years, it's worth considering their long-term value to the company. Now, this doesn't necessarily mean termination; it simply suggests they might not reach their full potential or become top performers in their current role.

Things get even more interesting when the organization itself experiences growth. Imagine that same employee – they might be perfectly suited for their current position, but what happens if the company's needs evolve? Perhaps the technology changes or the skillset required for the role expands. In such situations, the onus falls on both the employer and the employee to ensure continuous development.

As leaders, it's our responsibility to provide our employees with the necessary training and resources to keep pace with the organization's growth. However, employees can't solely rely on the company for their professional development. Taking the initiative and seeking out opportunities for personal growth is equally important.

Now, the real challenge arises when the situation flips. What happens if the organization, or the job itself, has significantly evolved, and the employee hasn't kept up? In my experience, the kindest and most productive course of action might be to let that individual go. This might sound harsh, but as someone who's managed teams and departments, I firmly believe in building the strongest possible team. Letting go of someone who can no longer contribute effectively allows you to bring in someone who possesses the necessary skills to help the organization thrive.

A Lesson Learned: The Unexpected Benefit of Termination

I once had to make the difficult decision to terminate an employee. He was a well-liked individual with a strong understanding of the business, and everyone knew him within the organization. Unfortunately, his skills and approach were no longer aligned with the company's evolving needs.

On the day of termination, we sat down for a private conversation outside. I explained my reasoning and the rationale behind the decision. While he was initially upset and left angrily, a surprising turn of events unfolded.

A week later, the same employee returned to my office, expressing his gratitude. He admitted that being let go was the wake-up call he needed. It prompted him to take a step back and re-evaluate his career path.

This experience highlights the importance of respectful termination procedures. When delivering the news, avoid comparing the employee to a potential replacement. Focus on clear communication and maintain a professional demeanor. There's no need to make the individual feel belittled or inadequate.

Avoiding Excuses: When Letting Go is the Right Choice

One of the most common excuses I hear from managers hesitant to terminate an employee is the individual's perceived importance. They might reason that the employee is simply too critical to the team at that moment or that the workload is already overwhelming.

However, in my experience, these justifications often hold little water. If an employee is no longer a good fit, or their skillset can't keep pace with the evolving role, their perceived importance becomes irrelevant. As a leader, it's crucial to prioritize effective management and make decisions that benefit the long-term health of the organization. I've never regretted letting someone go too soon; on the contrary, the most frequent regret I hear from managers is waiting too long to address a performance issue.

Here's another factor to consider: the impact on the remaining team members. Believe me, if you're seeing performance issues, chances are your team is too. Letting go of someone who isn't contributing effectively can actually be a positive step. It allows the rest of the team to step up, take ownership, and potentially even feel relieved that the situation has finally been addressed. You might even hear them ask why it took so long and how they can help during the transition period.

The bottom line is this: if an employee is no longer aligned with the organization's needs or the role has grown beyond their capabilities, the most ethical and productive course of action might be to let them go. Of course, this process should always be handled with respect and professionalism.

Termination: Delivering the News with Respect and Empathy

One of the most valuable pieces of advice I've received regarding termination is to keep the meeting brief and prioritize active listening. Letting someone go is a difficult situation, so avoid prolonging the conversation or feeling pressured to fill the silence.

The meeting should take place in a private and neutral space, such as your office or a conference room. Start by directly stating the purpose of the meeting. For example, you could say, "Paul, I've called you in today to inform you that this will be your last day at XYZ."

When the reason for termination is a layoff or company restructuring, ensure the employee understands they are not being singled out for performance issues. Conversely, if the termination is due to a policy violation, clearly explain the specific violation that led to this decision.

In my experience, employees typically react in one of two ways. Many will shut down and become silent. Having been terminated myself, I can relate to this reaction. The immediate concerns are overwhelming – your family, finances, job search – and silence becomes a way to process those emotions. In such cases, it's important to avoid rambling or over-explaining the situation. The employee is likely not absorbing the additional information.

The other potential reaction is for the employee to become defensive and question the decision. While understandable, avoid getting drawn into a lengthy debate. You can calmly state, "At this point, the decision is final. I encourage you to take some time to focus on moving forward. I'm happy to meet with you after hours if you need help packing your belongings, or we can arrange for someone to assist you."

The most important takeaway, regardless of the situation, is to maintain respect and empathy. Remember, termination is a stressful event, and the employee is likely experiencing a range of difficult emotions. Being respectful and understanding goes a long way in navigating this challenging process.

The Inevitable Turnover: When CEOs Get Let Go

Being a CEO comes with a unique set of challenges, one of which is the likelihood of being fired at some point. While misconduct is an obvious reason for termination, I'm focusing here on situations where the departure stems from differences in opinion, strategic direction, or leadership styles.

In my experience, every serial CEO I know has faced termination at least once. It's important to clarify that this doesn't involve situations like ethical lapses or illegal behavior. These are instances where the CEO and the board simply disagree on the company's future or how to manage it.

The Sting of Termination

Yes, I've been fired myself. For CEOs, the euphemisms tend to be creative – "stepping down for personal reasons" or "pursuing other ventures." The reality? It can feel like having a Band-Aid ripped off unexpectedly. It's a painful experience, and no amount of consolation can truly ease the initial sting.

However, looking back on these experiences (yes, there have been more than one!), I can confidently say they were ultimately positive developments. Each time, it led to new doors opening, presenting bigger and better opportunities. In hindsight, it's clear that both the board and I were unhappy with the situation, and a change was necessary. These terminations, though difficult at the time, ultimately served as a springboard for a brighter future.

The Importance of Growth: When Letting Go Can Be a Positive Step

During my time as a mentor, a business owner once confided in me about a key employee, someone she considered a co-founder and vital partner. This individual had been instrumental in the company's success over the past decade. However, her concern was that the employee seemed stagnant and unhappy. He was constantly requesting more responsibility, a larger salary, increased ownership, and a more prominent role within the company.

While it might seem harsh, my advice to her was to consider letting this employee go. This might sound counterintuitive, but in my experience, it could be the most beneficial course of action for the employee's long-term growth.

As employees, we thrive on challenges; they are the catalysts for our professional development. A manager I once had offered sage advice: "If you're not experiencing occasional butterflies in your stomach throughout your career, it's a sign you need to move on. The lack of challenge indicates stagnation."

The employee I mentioned earlier was undeniably talented and well-compensated. However, he had reached a point of comfort within the company, and there were limited opportunities for him to be challenged and grow further. The owner simply couldn't offer him the level of advancement he craved unless she was willing to step aside.

The decision to let someone go can be painful, similar to ripping off a Band-Aid. It will undoubtedly affect the business owner as well, but I firmly believe the employee would eventually express gratitude for this push. He would eventually recognize that his comfort zone had become a barrier to growth and that he might never have left on his own initiative. Perhaps this is why mother birds nudge their young out of the nest – it's a necessary step for them to learn to fly.

Recognizing When It's Time to Move On A Salesperson's Story

Earlier, I discussed the concept of "firing yourself" – taking the initiative to leave a comfortable position and pursue new challenges. This concept resonated with a close friend, a highly successful salesperson with an impressive track record at his networking hardware company for 15 years. His expertise in the industry, customer base, competitors, and products was unparalleled.

He contacted me, unsure of his next step. When I asked for clarification, he mentioned seeking a raise, ownership opportunities, and a more lucrative commission plan. However, my advice was to consider leaving the company altogether. In essence, it was time for him to "fire himself."

His performance wasn't the issue; he consistently topped sales figures. What he craved was growth, challenge, and that pre-challenge excitement. I was certain he hadn't experienced true sales call jitters in a long time. More money or a better commission plan wouldn't address this underlying need.

This situation highlights the importance of recognizing when it's time to move on. If you find yourself longing for new challenges and opportunities for professional development, don't be afraid to step outside your comfort zone and pursue them. Leaving a secure position can be daunting, but it can also be the most empowering decision you make for your career.

The Impact on Those Who Remain

Throughout this discussion on termination, it's important to remember the impact this process can have on the remaining employees. While letting someone go might be necessary, the decision shouldn't be taken lightly, particularly in situations of large-scale layoffs.

I can speak from experience on this. I once led a company that made the difficult decision to lay off nearly half its workforce. Federal regulations mandated that we provide 60 days' notice before the layoffs took effect.

Telling nearly 50% of our employees they would be losing their jobs within two months was incredibly challenging. This period was understandably difficult for everyone, but especially for those who remained. They might have felt a sense of guilt about keeping their jobs or hesitant to express joy about staying. The workload also increased significantly as departing employees were understandably granted time off for job interviews.

This experience underscores the importance of considering the impact of termination on the entire team, not just the individual being let go.

Steve Jobs' quote, "It turned out that getting fired from Apple was the best thing that could have ever happened to me. The heaviness of being successful was replaced by the lightness of being a beginner again," perfectly captures the message conveyed in this chapter.

Just as Jobs' termination propelled him towards greater innovation, sometimes letting an employee go, though difficult, can be a catalyst for positive change. This chapter explored the complexities of termination, from navigating the decision-making process to ensuring a respectful and empathetic approach. It also highlighted the importance of considering the impact on both the departing employee and the remaining team. Ultimately, termination, when handled thoughtfully, can serve as a springboard for new opportunities and growth for all parties involved.

Chapter Eleven
Lessons From Leadership:
The Good And The Bad

"Good managers can provide valuable lessons on effective leadership, communication, and management skills. They can serve as role models for how to lead a team, build morale, and achieve goals.

Bad managers, on the other hand, can provide valuable lessons on what not to do as a leader. By observing bad managers, you can learn how to handle difficult situations and people more effectively."

— Trevor Johnson

I am truly grateful for the remarkable career and life I've been fortunate to experience. Throughout my professional journey, I've had the privilege of collaborating with exceptional organizations and talented individuals. These enriching experiences have taken me to all corners of the globe, allowing me to work and travel internationally.

While I've previously expressed my appreciation for the guidance and support I've received from phenomenal mentors, leaders, and advisors, I must also acknowledge the valuable lessons learned from working alongside some truly ineffective managers. These experiences, though challenging, have provided invaluable insights into the qualities that define a truly great leader.

In my experience, ineffective leadership can be just as impactful as strong leadership, albeit in a different way. Trevor Johnson, writing for US Bank in a 2023 LinkedIn article titled "Learning More from Bad Managers," perfectly captures this sentiment. He argues that bad managers can teach us valuable lessons, specifically what not to do. I wholeheartedly agree.

Throughout my career, I've witnessed firsthand the detrimental effects of poor management practices. These include leaders who suffer from "analysis paralysis," becoming immobilized by the fear of making a decision. They hesitate to take action, even on seemingly routine matters. Equally damaging is the tendency to blame employees for mistakes.

This fosters a culture of fear and discourages honest communication. Conversely, strong leaders take ownership of both successes and failures, recognizing that setbacks are opportunities for growth.

Another red flag is the unwillingness to seek advice or help. Effective leaders understand that they don't have all the answers and that collaboration is key to success. A manager who talks excessively and fails to listen actively stifles innovation and dampens employee morale. The most effective leaders prioritize active listening, encouraging open communication, and fostering a sense of trust within the team.

Finally, disrespect towards employees is a fundamental failure of leadership. A manager who belittles or undervalues their team members will ultimately create a toxic work environment.

These negative experiences have significantly shaped my own approach to leadership. I believe that being a manager is a privilege, not a right. It comes with a responsibility to guide and support your team, to create an environment where employees feel valued and empowered to reach their full potential.

If you are not prepared to embrace these responsibilities, then leadership is not for you. Having witnessed the toll that bad management takes on employee morale and overall productivity, I am committed to leading by example.

Habits of Great Managers

Effective leadership is not about wielding authority; it's about fostering an environment where individuals can thrive. The best managers share a set of core practices that contribute to a positive and productive team dynamic. In this section, I'd like to delve into these habits and explain how they translate into real-world leadership.

1. Decisive Action with Flexibility

One of my biggest pet peeves is what I call "analysis paralysis." It's the tendency for some managers to become immobilized by the fear of making a wrong decision. They endlessly analyze every possible scenario and outcome, ultimately delaying action altogether. While careful consideration is important, there's a difference between thoughtful planning and debilitating indecision.

The key lies in striking a balance. Great leaders gather as much information as possible before making a choice. However, they understand that perfect information is often an illusion. Sometimes, the best course of action is to make a decision based on the available data, knowing you can always adjust course if necessary.

Being an effective leader means being action-oriented. Don't shy away from making decisions. However, also be prepared to admit when you've made a mistake. The ability to course-correct is a hallmark of strong leadership.

This leads us to the next essential habit:

2. Taking Ownership and Protecting Your Team

Mistakes are inevitable in any workplace. As a manager, you will make decisions that don't pan out as expected, your team members will encounter challenges, and unforeseen circumstances will arise. The important thing is how you handle these situations.

Truly exceptional managers understand the concept of ownership. They take responsibility for their team's failures. They won't hesitate to step up and take the blame for shortcomings, protecting their employees from undue criticism or blame. When something goes wrong, the focus should be on learning and improvement, not scapegoating individuals.

This concept extends beyond just shielding your team from blame. Great managers actively create an environment where employees feel safe taking calculated risks and trying new things. Fear of failure can be a paralyzing force, and fostering a culture of open communication and learning allows for innovation and growth.

Here's a personal anecdote that exemplifies the opposite approach: I once encountered an executive who seemed to take perverse pleasure in finding fault. Nothing escaped his critical eye, whether it be the lunch at a manager meeting or the font used in a presentation. His constant negativity created a stifling atmosphere, and morale among his employees was demonstrably low.

Let's be clear: mistakes are going to happen. Great managers understand this and use these experiences as opportunities for growth, not as ammunition for criticism.

3.   Seeking Help and Advice as a Strength

No one is expected to know everything. Even the most experienced managers will encounter situations outside their expertise. The key differentiator here is the willingness to seek help or advice when needed.

I vividly remember a member of one of my former boards. He was a sales force of nature, with decades of experience and an undeniable knack for closing deals. When concerns arose regarding the company's sales performance, he was brought on board with the expectation that he would share his expertise. However, despite being there for over a year, the CEO never once reached out to him for guidance or advice. This struck me as a tremendous waste of resources.

Effective managers recognize that seeking help is not a sign of weakness; it's a sign of strength and good judgment. Tapping into the knowledge and experience of others can lead to better decision-making and improved outcomes. Don't be afraid to ask questions, solicit feedback, and learn from those around you. Remember, you don't have to accept every suggestion that comes your way, but demonstrating a willingness to listen and learn is crucial.

4. Active Listening

Have you ever worked for a manager who seemed obsessed with talking about themselves and their accomplishments? This is a classic sign of insecurity. True leadership focuses on empowering your team, not singing your own praises.

The best managers I've had the privilege of working with are remarkably humble. They rarely boast about their achievements and are genuinely interested in hearing the ideas and perspectives of others. They actively listen, ask thoughtful questions, and encourage a collaborative environment where everyone feels comfortable contributing.

Here's a simple test you can apply to your own leadership style: at your next team meeting, pay attention to how much you're speaking compared to your team members. If you find yourself dominating the conversation, it's a strong signal that you need to step back and listen more. Effective communication is a two-way street, and fostering open dialogue is essential for building trust and a strong team dynamic.

5. Demonstrating Appreciation

One of the most crucial aspects of effective leadership is fostering a sense of value and appreciation within your team. Employees who feel valued are more engaged, productive, and loyal. Here, I'd like to share some practical strategies that I've found to be particularly effective in achieving this goal.

6. Treat Employees with Respect

Before even considering specific actions, it's essential to establish a fundamental principle: treat your employees with the same respect and courtesy you would extend to a valued business partner. Your position as a manager doesn't entitle you to treat your team members with anything less than respect. Imagine how you would interact with someone you consider an equal collaborator and translate that approach into your daily interactions with your team.

7. Eradicate Entitlement

There's nothing more demoralizing for an employee than encountering a manager who wields their position as a weapon. Phrases like "Do you know who I am?" or variations that leverage status or perceived importance are not only unprofessional but also create a hostile work environment.

I recall an incident that perfectly exemplifies this behavior. Early in my academic career, I witnessed a university official berating a young employee at a hotel front desk. The official's sense of entitlement was palpable, and her attempt to leverage her position to gain special treatment was not only ineffective but also deeply disrespectful.

Remember, your employees are the backbone of your organization. They deserve to be treated with dignity and courtesy, regardless of their role.

8. Simple Gestures, Profound Impact

Now that we've established a foundation of respect, let's explore some practical ways to show your team that you value them. While financial compensation and benefits are important, true appreciation goes beyond these tangible rewards. Here are five simple yet powerful strategies:

- Performance Reviews: Conduct annual performance reviews that go beyond just the potential for a raise. Take the time to provide detailed feedback, highlighting both an employee's strengths and areas for improvement. This demonstrates your commitment to their professional development.

- Regular One-on-One: Schedule regular one-on-one meetings with each team member. This dedicated time allows for focused conversation about their work, projects, and any challenges they may be facing. Equally important, it provides an opportunity for them to offer feedback on your leadership style.

- Personalized Notes: The power of a handwritten note cannot be understated. Take the time to write a personalized note on an employee's birthday and work anniversary. A simple gesture of recognition goes a long way in demonstrating that you see and appreciate their contributions.

- Lunch Dates: Remember how much it meant to you early in your career when a supervisor took you to lunch? Recreate that experience by inviting your team members to lunch occasionally. This allows for informal conversation and helps build stronger relationships within the team.

- Acknowledge and Greet: Make a conscious effort to acknowledge and greet your employees throughout the day. A simple "hello" or a brief conversation demonstrates that you value them as individuals, not just cogs in the machine.

One strategy I heard from a friend involved a general manager who carried a $100 bill. If he passed an employee without acknowledging them, they were entitled to the money. While the financial incentive is a bit extreme, the underlying message is clear: your employees deserve your recognition and respect.

9. Prioritizing Employee Wellbeing

Effective leadership isn't just about achieving results; it's about creating an environment where your team can thrive. This means prioritizing the well-being of your employees and fostering a sense of mutual respect and support.

10. Employees: Your Most Valuable Asset

Some might argue that a company's primary focus should be on clients, customers, or the board of directors. While these stakeholders are important, I firmly believe that a strong foundation built on employee well-being is the cornerstone of any successful organization. When you prioritize the well-being of your team and strive to be a good manager, your employees, in turn, will go above and beyond to ensure the success of the company.

11. Leading with Positivity

We all experience bad days, but a truly effective leader shields their team from the negativity. There's no excuse for taking out your personal frustrations on your employees. Imagine an employee going home and saying, "Today was a good day because my manager was in a good mood." Contrast that with, "I don't know what was wrong, but my supervisor never spoke to me all day." The leader in the second scenario is creating a toxic environment.

If you can't separate your personal struggles from your professional demeanor, then leadership may not be the right path for you. Your employees deserve a manager who consistently projects a positive and supportive attitude.

12. Open Communication

It astounds me that some managers neglect to have regular, meaningful one-on-one conversations with their team members. Statements like "I talk to them every day" or "We're a small team, so we don't need one-on-ones" are simply excuses. Effective leadership requires a deeper connection with your employees.

Regular one-on-one meetings provide a dedicated space for focused conversation. Discuss their work, current projects, and any challenges they're facing. Equally important, give them a platform to express their thoughts on your leadership style and ask questions. Don't be the manager who has never had a one-on-one with their employees.

13. Taking a Genuine Interest

Employees are more than just cogs in a machine; they are individuals with aspirations, challenges, and personal lives. When you encounter them in the hallway, take a moment to acknowledge them by name. Ask how they're doing, and be genuinely interested in their response.

Earlier in this book, I discussed the leadership style of Jim Buckley at Apple. He exemplified the power of simply walking the halls and engaging with his employees. He wasn't just making small talk; he took the time to learn about their work, their families, and their well-being. His sincere concern for each individual fostered a sense of loyalty and mutual respect.

In conclusion, the impact of strong leadership on employee satisfaction and overall organizational success cannot be overstated. Great managers foster a positive work environment where individuals feel valued, respected, and empowered to contribute their best. They create a sense of team spirit and cultivate a culture of open communication.

Throughout this chapter, I've outlined a set of key habits that are hallmarks of effective leadership. I encourage both managers and employees to reflect on these practices and strive for continuous improvement.

Employees, remember that you have a voice. Use the outlined list of habits to hold your managers accountable for creating a positive and productive work environment where you can thrive.

As a final thought, I'd like to leave you with a powerful quote by Nora Denzel: "Having a bad boss isn't your fault. Staying with one is." Don't settle for an uninspiring or negative leadership environment. Seek out opportunities to work for someone who truly embodies the qualities of a great manager, someone who will empower you to grow and contribute to your full potential.

Chapter Twelve
Navigating Professional Gatherings With Preparation And Sobriety

"Be Prepared...the meaning of the motto is that a scout must prepare himself by previous thinking out and practicing how to act on any accident or emergency so that he is never taken by surprise."

-Robert Baden-Powell

The Boy Scout motto, "Be Prepared," resonated deeply with me during my scouting days. Having essentials like a poncho for rain or waterproof matches to start a fire was crucial. As I transitioned to a CEO role, I discovered that this principle held even greater importance. Several stressful experiences, which I'll share with you, solidified this belief.

Here's a concrete example of why being prepared is paramount. While serving as CEO of TurboLinux, I was invited to deliver the keynote address at the opening of Linux World in South Korea. Working collaboratively with my Vice President of Marketing at our San Francisco headquarters, we meticulously crafted a presentation that explored the current state of Linux and its projected future. Upon completion, the presentation was sent to our marketing team in South Korea.

Imagine my dismay when I arrived at the conference center two hours before my keynote speech, only to discover that my slides were nowhere to be found! Fortunately, I had brought a copy of the script and a portable drive containing several past presentations. While I managed to piece together a presentation, it didn't seamlessly integrate with the script due to the mismatch between slides and spoken content. Looking out at the audience, I saw attendees wearing headsets and listening to interpreters translate my English speech into Korean and Mandarin. I can only assume that when a slide didn't align with my spoken words, they simply attributed it to an interpreter error. This incident served as a pivotal lesson: never travel without a backup copy of your presentation on a thumb drive.

Not Solely Reliant on Technology

While I'm a big proponent of PowerPoint as a valuable tool for storytelling, lecturing, or group updates, I also learned the importance of not relying solely on prepared presentations. This lesson unfolded during my company's fundraising process, which involved pitching to various venture capital firms, technology investors, and corporate investors. These presentations typically outlined the organization, the problem it addressed, the market size, and the projected profitable market share we could capture.

One day, while waiting for my turn to present at a Sandhill Road firm in Palo Alto, thumb drive in hand, I was ushered into a conference room where eight firm representatives sat around a large, beautiful wooden table. Anticipating the presentation, I raised my thumb drive and inquired about where to connect it. To my surprise, the reply came, "No PowerPoint, please. Just tell us what you were going to present." Thankfully, having delivered the presentation for weeks, I knew it inside and out. The presentation flowed smoothly, and ultimately, they became an investor. However, this experience highlighted the importance of being prepared to present without relying on slides or technology. You may encounter situations where technical difficulties or malfunctioning AV equipment prevent you from using your prepared presentation. Being adaptable and comfortable presenting without visuals is key.

Alcohol and Performance

While I can't cite specific data, in my personal experience, I've never witnessed a positive business outcome facilitated by alcohol. In fact, I've seen the opposite occur all too often: careers shattered, deals falling apart, and job offers rescinded, all due to alcohol use.

It's important to clarify that I'm not referring to the occasional celebratory toast with champagne, a glass of wine with a management team dinner, or even a drink at a company holiday party.

Being under the influence or anything less than 100% mentally sharp is a recipe for disaster in a business setting. For this reason, I rarely drink in any business-related situation, including company parties. This philosophy proved challenging when running companies internationally, particularly in cultures where business is often conducted after hours over meals and drinks. On such occasions, I would often resort to the excuse of taking medication that couldn't be mixed with alcohol.

Alcohol and the Interview Process

A close friend of mine who ran a large tech company in Florida had a unique interview strategy. Each year, they would recruit from the latest MBA graduating class. Top candidates were invited to spend a day on a chartered yacht with an open bar and plentiful food. While the candidates were encouraged to relax and enjoy themselves, it was also an unspoken test to see who would overindulge. The rationale was that if someone got drunk during an interview process, how could they be expected to maintain professionalism when out with clients or representing the company in social settings?

My friend recounted stories every year about candidates who drank excessively and even became sick on the yacht. Needless to say, those individuals were never offered positions.

While I have never personally encountered this specific interview tactic, I have had board members during my interview processes invite me to dinner or drinks, insisting that "tonight's on us, so drink up." In these situations, I politely declined, explaining that I preferred to maintain a clear head throughout the interview process.

Leading by Example: Professionalism Matters

As a leader, your conduct sets the tone for the entire organization. This principle extends to company parties, where maintaining professionalism is paramount. While fostering a fun and celebratory environment is important, indulging in alcohol to the point of intoxication can send the wrong message and undermine your authority. Remember, you are a role model, and your behavior has a significant impact on your employees.

Leaders Celebrate with Associates, Not Before Them

True leadership involves celebrating successes with your team, not ahead of them. Allow your employees to enjoy themselves and unwind at company parties. Your role is to be present, create a positive atmosphere, and show your appreciation for their hard work. Of course, this doesn't preclude you from having a drink or two, but moderation is key. The focus should be on creating a fun and memorable experience for your team, not on your own personal enjoyment.

The 24/7 CEO: Always Representing the Company

In my experience, a CEO's responsibility extends beyond traditional business hours. As the head of the organization, you are, in a sense, a constant representative of the company. This means maintaining a professional demeanor in all settings, not just during work hours. This doesn't require you to be uptight or devoid of personality but rather to conduct yourself with a level of maturity and responsibility that reflects your position.

Ultimately, by prioritizing professionalism in all aspects of your leadership, you gain the respect and appreciation of your employees. They will recognize your commitment to excellence and your dedication to the organization's success. This, in turn, fosters a positive and productive work environment where everyone feels valued and empowered to contribute their best.

The significance of readiness, which I have stressed throughout this conversation, is aptly captured by the Robert Baden-Powell quotation, "Be Prepared...the meaning of the motto is that a scout must prepare himself by previous thinking out and practicing how to act on any accident or emergency so that he is never taken by surprise."

Success in business depends on being ready for unforeseen circumstances, just as a scout foresees obstacles and provides himself with the required instruments. Adopting the spirit of preparedness found in the Scout Motto is essential to becoming a good leader, from making backup presentations to acting professionally in social situations.

Chapter Thirteen
Mastering The Interview: Impress Without Crossing Boundaries

"If you are insecure, guess what? The rest of the world is too. Do not overestimate the competition and underestimate yourself. You are better than you think."

-T. Harv Eker

In my tenure as a CEO, which typically spanned two years per company, I frequently participated in interviews on both sides of the table. My role often involved taking startups to the next level, which could encompass various outcomes such as acquisitions, mergers, initial public offerings (IPOs), or even closures. This extensive experience has equipped me with a unique perspective on the interview process.

While many individuals find interviews to be stressful experiences, I've always viewed them in a positive light. With a deeper understanding of the interview process and what organizations typically seek in candidates, the interview can transform from a nerve-wracking event into a valuable opportunity.

Being shortlisted for an interview is a significant accomplishment that deserves a confidence boost. It indicates that your resume and cover letter have successfully conveyed your qualifications and piqued the hiring manager's interest. Most organizations wouldn't expend their time interviewing candidates who lack the essential skills and experience for the position.

Approaching the interview with this understanding can significantly reduce pre-interview jitters. At this stage, the focus has shifted from assessing basic qualifications to determining which qualified candidate would be the best fit for the role and the company culture. Interviewers are looking for someone who will work harmoniously with the board of directors, collaborate effectively with the team, and garner the support of investors.

In my experience, success often hinged on authenticity. By confidently presenting my true personality and work style, I could demonstrate whether I would be a compatible addition to the team. Keeping this in mind simplifies the interview process; it becomes a chance to showcase your strengths and determine if the company aligns with your goals and values. This shift in perspective can transform the interview into a positive and mutually beneficial experience.

Throughout this chapter, I'll share my top tips to help you navigate the interview process and make a lasting impression.

1. The First Impression: A Lasting Impact

The very first moments of an interview hold immense weight. They set the tone for the entire interaction and can significantly influence the interviewer's perception of you. Remember, you've already cleared the initial hurdle by being selected for an interview. Now, the focus shifts to determining if you'd be a good fit for the role, the team, and the company culture. This is where a strong first impression becomes crucial.

- The Power of Punctuality and Preparation:

Your punctuality speaks volumes about your professionalism and respect for the interviewer's time. Avoid the temptation to park in the closest spot. Instead, choose a space further away. This allows you a few moments to collect yourself, take a deep breath, and mentally prepare for the interview.

Treat everyone with courtesy, from the receptionist who greets you to the interviewer themselves. A genuine smile and a polite introduction go a long way in creating a positive first impression. In my experience, receptionists often share their observations of candidates with the hiring manager. Make sure yours is a positive one!

- Planning Makes Perfect:

Plan to arrive at least 10 minutes before your scheduled interview time. This demonstrates your respect for the interviewer's schedule and allows you a buffer in case of unforeseen delays. Introduce yourself to the receptionist and inform them of your appointment.

While waiting, avoid the urge to slouch in a chair. Stand tall and project confidence. You can use this time to briefly review your notes or a magazine to keep yourself occupied. However, silence your phone completely – a ringing phone during the interview is a major faux pas.

- Professional Attire: Always a Safe Bet

Dressing professionally is an essential element of making a strong first impression. For some college students, navigating professional attire can be tricky. A black shirt and white tie might seem like a formal choice, but it falls short in an interview setting.

For men, a conservative black, gray, or dark blue suit is a safe bet. Pair it with a crisp, white, ironed cotton shirt and a classic silk tie. Polish your black leather shoes to complete the polished look. Women can opt for a conservative black, gray, or dark blue suit or dress with a blazer. A light-colored blouse or shirt underneath adds a touch of professionalism.

- Casual Culture, Formal Approach:

Even if the company culture leans towards casual attire, it's always advisable to err on the side of formality for the interview. A suit demonstrates that you take the opportunity seriously and are committed to making a good impression.

If the interviewer specifically instructs you to dress casually, you can explain your choice of attire. A simple statement like, "This opportunity is very important to me, and I wanted to make a professional impression," conveys your respect for the company and the interview process.

- The Importance of Personal Presentation:

Beyond attire, take a moment to ensure your overall presentation is polished. My son once applied for a valet job, and I advised him to wear a suit despite the company's casual environment. He argued that a suit wouldn't be necessary for a job where he'd be running around the parking lot. However, he ended up getting hired on the spot precisely because he was the only candidate who dressed professionally.

Invest in a thin leather portfolio to carry your resume and notes. Ensure your resume is printed on high-quality heavyweight paper in white, pale white, or gray. While electronic tablets can be used, keep them in a portfolio with a dedicated pocket for your resume.

- The Final Touches:

Finally, don't underestimate the importance of good personal hygiene. Brush your teeth and pop a breath mint before the interview to ensure a fresh and professional demeanor. By following these simple yet impactful tips, you can ensure a strong first impression that sets the stage for a successful interview.

2. Research the Company: Knowledge is Power

Demonstrating a thorough understanding of the company you're interviewing with goes a long way in creating a positive impression. It shows initiative, genuine interest, and a commitment to the opportunity. The most common interview question – "What do you know about our company?" – highlights the importance of conducting thorough research.

During a guest lecture at my alma mater, a local bank executive shared a startling statistic: a staggering 80% of the candidates she interviewed appeared completely unprepared, lacking basic knowledge about the bank. To stand out from the crowd, approach your research with the same dedication you would a major exam.

- Equipping Yourself with Knowledge:

Your research should delve into the company's core aspects. Learn about their founding story, their primary products or services, the number of offices and employees, and their geographical footprint. Recent announcements and company news are also valuable areas to explore.

- Striking the Right Balance:

However, there's a fine line between thorough research and excessive creepiness. In one instance, while interviewing a candidate for a Sales VP position, I was taken aback when he proceeded to disclose my past work history and even the names of my wife and children. Let's emphasize this point – your research should be limited to publicly available information about the company itself.

- Leveraging Technology:

The internet serves as your research treasure trove. Don't simply rely on the company's website – delve deeper! Take the time to write down key facts and jot down notes as you gather information. While you likely won't refer to these notes during the interview itself, the act of writing them down helps solidify the information in your memory.

- Maintaining a Positive Focus:

It's important to maintain a positive and professional demeanor throughout your research. Avoid dwelling on any negative news or unflattering information you may encounter about the company. The last thing you want to do is raise red flags by mentioning a recent DUI arrest of the CEO or any other potentially damaging details.

3. Ask Insightful Questions: Turning the Tables

The interview is a two-way street. While the interviewer assesses your qualifications, you also have the opportunity to evaluate the company culture and determine if the role aligns with your goals. This is where your portfolio comes in handy.

- Prepare Your Questions:

Don't be caught off guard when the interviewer asks if you have any questions. A simple "No, I think you've covered everything" conveys a lack of initiative and interest. Instead, come prepared with a list of thoughtful questions. This demonstrates your engagement and commitment to understanding the opportunity further.

- Beyond Compensation:

While compensation and benefits are important factors, avoid asking about them during the initial interview. Focus on questions that delve deeper into the company, the role itself, and the interviewer's experience.

- Turning the Tables:

Frame your questions in a way that "turns the tables" and allows you to learn more about the company culture. For instance, you could ask about the interviewer's tenure at the company, what they enjoy most about their role, or what specific actions helped them achieve success. You could also inquire about the biggest challenges associated with the position and how they personally addressed them.

- Genuine Curiosity is Key:

Remember, the key to effective questioning lies in sincerity and genuine interest. Don't ask questions simply for the sake of asking. Be present in the moment and actively listen to the interviewer's responses.

4. Conquering the Curveball: Answering Unusual Interview Questions

Interview questions can sometimes take unexpected turns. You might encounter unconventional inquiries like "If you were a cereal box, what would you be?" or "What kind of tree would you best resemble?" While these questions might seem bizarre, there's often a method to the madness.

- Humor as a Defense Mechanism:

For these more whimsical questions, consider using humor as a tool to diffuse the tension and showcase your personality. Remember, a shared laugh can go a long way in creating a positive rapport with the interviewer. Instead of offering a predictable response like "I'm an eagle, soaring high in the organization," use your creativity to craft a witty reply.

- Technical Challenges: Showcasing Your Thought Process

If you're interviewing for a technical position, you might encounter brain teasers like "How many marbles could fit in a Boeing 747?" or "Why are manhole covers round?" These questions aren't necessarily about finding the one "correct" answer. Instead, they're designed to assess your problem-solving approach and communication skills.

- Think Out Loud and Leverage Resources:

During these technical inquiries, verbalize your thought process. Explain how you would approach the problem, what factors you'd consider, and the steps you would take to arrive at a solution. If possible, inquire whether you can utilize a whiteboard to visually represent your thought process. This allows you to demonstrate your critical thinking skills and ability to communicate complex ideas effectively.

- A Personal Anecdote:

Fortunately, the most unusual question I encountered during my career came during a lunch interview with a technical founder who was interviewing me for the CEO position. He unexpectedly handed me a pencil and challenged me to sell it to him. Later, he admitted he felt unsure of how to interview me and had read this tactic in a book. Thankfully, my response must have been persuasive, as he offered me the job!

This experience highlights the importance of focusing on your thought process and problem-solving skills when faced with unusual interview questions. Remember, it's not always about providing the "right" answer – it's about demonstrating your ability to think critically, adapt to unexpected situations, and communicate effectively under pressure.

5. The Unexpected Request: A Tour for the Curious Mind

Standing out in a crowded interview pool requires initiative and a genuine interest in the opportunity. One unique tactic I've found effective is requesting a tour of the company's facilities at the conclusion of the interview.

- A Simple Yet Powerful Inquiry:

In 1983, during a college recruitment interview with a large manufacturing company, I concluded the conversation with an unexpected request: "Would you mind giving me a tour of the plant?" The interviewer, visibly surprised, remarked that in his four years of experience, no candidate had ever asked for a tour. By the end of that week, I received a job offer.

- Beyond the Factory Floor:

This tactic transcends manufacturing environments. Regardless of the industry, expressing a desire to see the workspace demonstrates your genuine curiosity and commitment to the opportunity. For instance, you could inquire about seeing the department you'd be working in, a specific team area, or any aspect of the company that piqued your interest during the interview.

- My Son's Experience:

My son's best friend, upon graduating from law school, was interviewing for a summer clerkship with a federal judge. When he sought my advice, I encouraged him to request a tour of the courthouse. He initially hesitated, believing there wasn't much to see beyond courtrooms. However, he ultimately followed my suggestion and landed the job!

- Making the Most of the Tour:

The key to a successful tour request lies in sincerity and a thirst for knowledge. During the tour, actively engage by asking insightful questions. This further demonstrates your enthusiasm and desire to learn more about the company culture and day-to-day operations. By taking this initiative, you can set yourself apart from other candidates and showcase your genuine interest in the opportunity.

6. The Importance of References: Choosing Wisely

Securing a job offer often hinges on a crucial step – the reference check. Here are some key considerations to ensure your references provide a positive and impactful endorsement.

- Seeking Consent:

Always, always ask for permission before listing someone as a reference. Respect their time and demonstrate courtesy by directly inquiring, "I'm interviewing with [Company Name], and they require three references. Would you be willing to provide me with a positive recommendation?" Most former colleagues or managers will appreciate you seeking their consent and may even offer valuable insights on what aspects of your experience to highlight. Whenever someone asks me to be a reference, I always inquire if there's anything specific I can emphasize to support their candidacy.

- Beyond the Obvious:

Be aware that some companies conduct in-depth reference checks. While they'll likely receive glowing reviews from your listed references, the interviewer might also reach out to additional individuals not on your list. This could include former colleagues or even someone from your previous employer who wasn't directly mentioned as a reference.

- Choosing Your Champions:

The selection of your references plays a critical role. Strive to include individuals who can speak directly to your skills, work ethic, and contributions within the context of the specific opportunity you're pursuing. For instance, when possible, prioritize listing former managers over peers. Managers have a more comprehensive understanding of your accomplishments and leadership capabilities.

- Avoiding Red Flags:

Omitting your most recent employer can raise red flags for potential employers. Similarly, listing a peer instead of a supervisor or someone outside the immediate work environment could raise questions. If you held leadership positions like CEO or President, avoid listing board members as references - focus on direct reports or managers who can provide a detailed account of your performance.

By following these tips and choosing your references carefully, you can ensure that the reference check plays a positive role in solidifying your candidacy and securing the job offer.

Conclusion:

Throughout this guide, I've shared a collection of tips gleaned from my extensive experience on both sides of the interview table. While I can't guarantee a job offer every time, I firmly believe that incorporating these strategies will significantly enhance your candidacy and help you stand out from the crowd.

These principles extend beyond the interview room and can be applied to other professional endeavors. For instance, the tactics discussed here can prove equally valuable when pursuing new business opportunities or attracting new clients for your sales goals.

A Final Encouragement:

By approaching interviews with confidence, thorough preparation, and genuine interest, you can transform them into positive and productive experiences. I wish you the very best of luck in your interviews and all your future endeavors.

The quote by T. Harv Eker, "If you are insecure, guess what? The rest of the world is too. Do not overestimate the competition and underestimate yourself. You are better than you think," perfectly encapsulates the message I've aimed to convey throughout this chapter. As you embark on your interview journey, approaching the process with confidence and self-belief is paramount.

Remember, many interviewers share similar anxieties about evaluating candidates. By following the interview tips and strategies outlined in this chapter, you can equip yourself with the tools and knowledge to not only impress interviewers but also assess if the company culture aligns with your own goals and aspirations. This transformation from interview anxiety to interview opportunity empowers you to take control of the experience and position yourself for success.

So, take a deep breath, believe in yourself, and confidently showcase your strengths and qualifications. Remember, the interview is a two-way street, and you are interviewing the company just as much as they are interviewing you. With the guidance offered here, you can navigate the interview process with confidence and emerge victorious in securing the opportunity that best suits your talents and aspirations.

Chapter Fourteen
Moving Bribes And Positional Realities

"A man should never neglect his family for business."

-Walt Disney

In reflecting on this book, which details the various factors that contributed to my journey as a serial CEO, a profound realization strikes me. While I've meticulously chronicled the influence of mentors, boards, and management teams – not to mention the occasional stroke of luck – I now recognize the most critical element behind my success: my family.

This chapter delves into the unwavering support system that has been my family throughout my career. It all began during my senior year of college when I met Jill, the woman who would become my wife. A year later, we embarked on our married life together. Five years after our wedding, our family welcomed Kayci, followed by Matt, and finally, Ross. Our lives unfolded much like any other family's – until my career path took an unexpected turn, propelling me into the world of serial CEOs.

The Impact Of Frequent Moves On Our Family

Our family life, while seemingly ordinary at first glance, was significantly impacted by the demands of my serial CEO career. The most notable consequence was the constant relocation – a reality that necessitated immense sacrifice from my wife and children.

One vivid example of this occurred during our time in Boston. We had purchased a house with a long driveway, prompting neighbors to recommend a snow removal service in preparation for harsh winters. The first winter proved mild, and despite the light snowfall, the service routinely showed up, much to our amusement.

However, the following winter presented a different story. Having accepted a new role as CEO for a pre-IPO technology company in San Jose, I relocated to an apartment there while Jill remained in Boston with the kids to ensure they could finish school and we could sell the house. This physical separation created challenges. During one phone call home, I naively bragged about the pleasant weather in San Jose. Kayci, answering the phone, informed me that Jill was stuck in the driveway, yet again, with a car buried in snow and a considerable amount of frustration. That winter saw record snowfall, and every time I returned home, I spent a significant amount of time shoveling, helping Jill navigate the winter chaos.

These constant moves were often met with resistance from the children, who understandably expressed their frustration at having to uproot their lives. Yet, Jill remained a pillar of support throughout my career. She expressed genuine happiness for my achievements and unwavering commitment to making our family life work despite the logistical complexities.

Impact On Children: The Price Of Mobility - "Moving Bribes"

The constant relocations not only strained our family dynamic but also significantly impacted my children. While Jill shouldered the logistical burdens, the emotional toll of these moves fell heavily on them. Witnessing their struggles became a turning point for me.

The initial strategy of using nicer houses as an incentive worked for the first few moves. However, a decision I made during our time in Tucson proved to be a turning point, introducing a complex dynamic I later dubbed "moving bribes."

As CEO of a Tucson-based company, we acquired several organizations in New Jersey and Boston. My vision was to pivot the company's focus to the technology developed by one of these acquisitions. This meant a move to Boston to oversee the transition. The board offered me a difficult choice: remain in Tucson and manage the existing business or relocate to Boston and spearhead the new venture.

For several months, I attempted a compromise, working in Boston while flying back to Tucson every two weeks for extended weekends. It was a challenging period, keeping me physically distant from both my work and my family.

During one of these visits, while shopping with Kayci (who was eight at the time) and Ross (five), I brought up the possibility of moving to Boston to be a family again. Kayci, clearly missing my presence, expressed her apprehension about another move. Determined to find a solution, I naively offered to get her something – anything – to change her mind. Her response was simple: "If I could have a dog, I would move."

Seized with relief, I readily agreed, promising a dog once we settled in Boston. However, what unfolded next highlighted the unintended consequences of my impulsive offer. As we continued shopping, I overheard Kayci, filled with newfound excitement, informing Ross about the upcoming move and her new dog. Generously, she extended the offer of a "moving gift" to him as well.

Ross, a passionate collector of Matchbox cars at the time, excitedly approached me, seeking confirmation. When I confirmed his sister's offer, he promptly declared his desire for a car (or perhaps two, after some negotiation with Kayci on the value of the "gift").

What began as a seemingly harmless attempt to ease the transition for my children quickly spiraled into a complex system of "moving bribes." As the children grew older, these bribes became more expensive and elaborate. They even developed a form of collective bargaining, strategizing together to maximize their rewards for each move.

Despite the "moving bribes" intended to soften the blow, our children undoubtedly made significant sacrifices to support my career. The constant relocations left a lasting impact on them. Someone once offered a poignant analogy, comparing them to trees – repeatedly uprooted and replanted, developing a remarkable ability to adapt but never truly establishing deep roots.

This reality was brought home to me when Kayci, reflecting on her life for her college admission essay, revealed the staggering number of 16 moves she had experienced in just 18 years. While all three of my children – Kayci, Matt, and Ross – have blossomed into successful individuals with fulfilling careers, I cannot ignore the sacrifices they made for my professional pursuits. The constant change undoubtedly shaped their lives in profound ways.

The Rock Of Our Family

Jill's unwavering support proved to be the bedrock of our family throughout this whirlwind period. Our relocation journey spanned a decade, taking us from Houston to San Francisco, Tucson, Boston, back to San Francisco, and finally, Tucson once again. The demands of my career often meant physically moving to a new location months before the rest of the family. This immense burden fell on Jill's shoulders. She shouldered the responsibility of selling our homes and managing the logistics of our moves, all while ensuring the well-being of our children during these transitions.

Guidance From Mentors

Throughout my career, I've been fortunate to receive invaluable advice from mentors who offered valuable perspectives. Two particular pieces of guidance stand out in my mind, each emphasizing the importance of family.

The first came from Ross Cooley, a respected figure in the industry. During a late-night flight back to Houston, we discussed the challenges of travel. While the specific details escape me, I vividly recall Ross cautioning me against excessive time away from home and family. His core message resonated deeply: nothing surpasses the significance of family. He emphasized the importance of not taking their unwavering support for granted, particularly in the face of frequent business travel.

The second piece of advice stemmed from Jerry Goldress, a consultant brought in by my board of directors early in my CEO tenure. Jerry offered a more practical suggestion for navigating family relocations. He believed the key to securing family buy-in for moves was to consistently upgrade their living situation. In essence, the new house should always be nicer than the previous one. While this strategy proved effective for the initial moves, it presented challenges when relocating from a place like Tucson to a significantly more expensive city like San Francisco. Despite the complexities, Jerry's core message – prioritizing family comfort during transitions – remained valuable.

Family: The Unsung Heroes Of My Success

Looking back, I am struck by a profound realization: despite the undeniable influence of mentors, boards, and even strokes of luck, none of it would have mattered without the unwavering support of my family. They are the true heroes of my story.

Jill, my wife, stands out as a pillar of strength. Her unwavering support formed the foundation upon which our family navigated the whirlwind of constant relocations. I am deeply grateful for her sacrifices and her unwavering commitment to keeping our family unit strong.

A pivotal moment of clarity came during a dinner with Ross Cooley. His reminder that he was approached because of his position as president of Compaq, not simply because he was Ross, resonated deeply. It echoed the sentiment I often expressed – that what truly matters is being a good husband and father. Family is the constant source of love and appreciation, independent of titles or professional achievements. They value you for who you are, not what you do.

The quote by Walt Disney, "A man should never neglect his family for business," perfectly encapsulates the central theme of this chapter. While chronicling the various factors that contributed to my success as a serial CEO, I've come to understand that none of it would have been possible without the unwavering support of my family.

This chapter has explored the impact of my career choices on my family. We endured the challenges of constant relocation, from the logistical burdens shouldered by Jill to the emotional toll it took on our children. Despite the "moving bribes" and other attempts to ease the transitions, their sacrifices were undeniable.

Yet, through it all, my family remained a constant source of strength. Jill's unwavering support served as the bedrock of our family, and the advice from mentors like Ross Cooley and Jerry Goldress emphasized the importance of prioritizing family.

In the end, the greatest takeaway from my career journey is not the accomplishments or accolades but the profound realization that true success is measured by the love and support of my family. They are, without a doubt, the unsung heroes of my story.

~~o~~

Chapter Fifteen
Charting The CEO's Course

"The price of success is hard work, dedication to the job at hand, and the determination that whether we win or lose, we have applied the best of ourselves to the task at hand."

-Vince Lombardi

In embarking on this book, my goal was to provide more than a simple list of instructions. I sought to share the nuances of my experiences through vivid details and illustrative anecdotes. This approach, I believe, offers a deeper understanding of the lessons learned throughout my career.

For this final chapter, I take a different approach. Here, I present a collection of fifteen key takeaways – a culmination of insights gleaned over the years. These lessons range from the practical to the profound, each one holding the potential to shape your professional journey as they have mine. While not presented in any specific order, I trust they will serve as valuable companions on your own path to success.

Lesson #1: Humility and Impact

One of the most important lessons I hope you will take away from this book is the concept of humility. True success is not measured by personal gain or outward achievements like titles, wealth, or possessions. It lies in the positive impact you make on the world around you.

This impact can be felt within your organization, on your team members and colleagues, and on the broader community of stakeholders you interact with. Strive to make a difference in the lives of those around you, be it through your work, your leadership, or simply by lending a helping hand.

Humility goes hand-in-hand with this concept. Throughout our lives, we are shaped and supported by a network of individuals. My own journey has been influenced by the guidance of my parents, teachers, mentors, and even fellow travelers. Expressing gratitude and acknowledging the contributions of others is a sign of strength, not weakness.

Earlier this year, I witnessed a powerful example of this principle. Dr. David Engelthaler, a highly accomplished professor and researcher, was awarded the prestigious title of Flagstaff Citizen of the Year. Dr. Engelthaler's dedication to public health is evident in his work leading a research team focused on advancing human health. His impressive credentials include published research and patented inventions.

Despite his achievements, Dr. Engelthaler's response to the award was one of remarkable humility. He deflected the spotlight, expressing his gratitude to his family, friends, and colleagues. He even went so far as to say that he didn't deserve the recognition alone. This selfless act perfectly embodies the spirit of "It isn't about you." Focus on the positive impact you can create, and let your actions speak for themselves.

Lesson #2: Navigating Negative Influences

While this book highlights the invaluable support I've received from mentors, managers, and friends throughout my career, it would be disingenuous to ignore the occasional negative influence. Just as sunshine accompanies rain, success can sometimes attract negativity.

I've encountered individuals whom I've chosen to call "Rays and Scotts" (after some past colleagues) who attempted to hinder my progress or spread negativity. These experiences, though fortunately not as frequent as the positive ones, offered valuable lessons.

In some cases, these negative interactions arose from seemingly positive beginnings. I offered mentorship and support to these individuals. However, their motivations shifted, and they began to work against me in subtle ways.

A mentor once dispensed a sage piece of advice: if universal popularity is your goal, leadership roles might not be the best fit. There will always be those who harbor dislike or envy for reasons often beyond your control.

I recall a specific instance early in my teaching career at Northern Arizona University. During lunch with my department chair, I was met with a blunt and discouraging remark. He questioned my qualifications and expressed confusion about my presence there.

These encounters can be disheartening, but it's important to remember that negativity is often rooted in insecurity. As you climb the ladder of success, there will inevitably be those who struggle with your achievements. Some might even resort to underhanded tactics.

The key is to not let these "Rays and Scotts" of the world derail you. They represent a small fraction of the people you'll encounter. Focus on the vast majority who will support and celebrate your success. Don't allow negativity to cloud your judgment, diminish your drive, or hinder your ability to develop and inspire others.

Lesson #3: Beyond Titles and Credentials

While this principle might resonate more with some than others, I believe it's important enough to include. It boils down to the concept of focusing on genuine connection over formalities.

There's a tendency to rely on titles and credentials as a badge of honor or a means of establishing authority. However, in most professional settings outside of academia or medicine, the constant use of titles like "Dr." can come across as pretentious or create unnecessary barriers.

I recall serving on a board alongside a chairperson who insisted on being addressed as "Doctor" despite his doctorate being in the education field. His business cards, office door, and all official correspondence prominently displayed the title.

In contrast, many of the brilliant professors I've encountered at Northern Arizona University actively discourage the use of "Dr." even though they hold PhDs. These are the same professors who refrain from including titles like "Dr." or "PhD" in their email signatures.

The same logic applies to designations like "MBA." There's little reason to include it on your business card, email signature, or everyday communication.

The underlying message here is that your value shouldn't be contingent on a string of initials or degrees. Your everyday work and interactions should naturally demonstrate your competence and expertise.

It's also worth noting that two of the most successful individuals I've known, both mentors and friends, never attended college. Their achievements stand as a testament to the power of hard work, talent, and perseverance.

Ultimately, what matters most is the human connection. We want to remember your name, not a collection of titles. And hopefully, you're not the kind of person who demands a formal title like "Mister," "President," or "Doctor" to be used in every interaction. Remember, as I've emphasized throughout this book, true success isn't about self-importance; it's about the impact you create.

Lesson #4: Embracing Cultural Nuances in Business Travel

My career has afforded me the privilege of extensive business travel, from domestic destinations across the United States to international locations like Japan, India, China, and various European countries. Early on, I recognized the importance of cultural awareness in building successful business relationships.

People hold a deep sense of pride in their hometowns, states, and countries. Taking the time to learn about the culture, history, political landscape, legal system, and language demonstrates respect and fosters rapport with your counterparts. Understanding local customs and norms, both in business and everyday life, is equally crucial.

For example, Japanese business etiquette dictates the exchange of gifts upon introduction. Imagine the potential faux pas of presenting a gift wrapped in white paper – a color associated with death in Japan – while receiving a gift from your counterpart. Furthermore, it's customary to express gratitude ("Arigato Gozaimasu") and set the received gift aside; it wouldn't be opened in the meeting itself.

These unique customs and perspectives exist across all countries and regions. Investing time to learn these nuances demonstrates genuine care for the relationship and fosters trust-building communication.

Lesson #5: Balancing Family and Business Travel

No one felt the sacrifices demanded by my CEO career more acutely than my three children. Early on, it wasn't uncommon for me to spend upwards of 75% of a month traveling. There were even periods when I worked on one coast while my family resided on the other.

One particularly difficult experience for us all was the aftermath of 9/11. While traveling for a fundraising event in London the night before, I witnessed the horrific attacks on the World Trade Center unfold on the news. Learning of the grounded air traffic only heightened the anxiety of my family back home, who were left wondering about my safety and return date for days.

In an effort to bridge the gap created by travel and foster an appreciation for other cultures in my children, I made a conscious effort to take them each on individual business trips. These trips included destinations closer to home, like New York City or Washington D.C., as well as more adventurous locations like Japan.

By the time my son Matt reached sixth grade, he was studying Japanese and had developed a remarkable level of proficiency. Imagine the surprise of our international colleagues upon encountering this young, blonde American boy conversing fluently in Japanese!

While these trips could never fully compensate for the time spent away, they did contribute to a deeper understanding of my work and an appreciation for the life we have in the United States. The lessons learned from these experiences resonate deeply, and I believe they offer valuable takeaways for anyone navigating the complexities of business travel and family life.

Lesson #6: The Power of a Handwritten Note

While I've mentioned this concept earlier, its significance warrants its inclusion in my top lessons. Make a habit of writing personalized notes. Invest in stationery with your name and use it to send brief messages of appreciation, congratulations or simply to stay connected.

We all cherish the act of receiving a handwritten note. It's a thoughtful gesture that evokes warmth and appreciation. The recipients of your notes can be anyone – your family, colleagues, or even someone you admire after reading about them in the news. Express gratitude, well wishes, or simply a desire to connect.

The motivation behind these notes shouldn't be self-serving or career-oriented. Sometimes, the most meaningful gestures are simply acts of kindness that brighten someone's day.

Lesson #7: Travel Efficiency – Loyalty Programs and Packing Tips

This lesson may seem like common sense, but it took me some time to fully grasp its value. As you embark on your business travel journey, strive for consistency by choosing preferred airlines, hotel chains, and car rental companies. While the initial allure of globetrotting at someone else's expense can be exciting, those feelings often wane over time.

In my younger years, I reveled in the novelty of travel. However, after years on the road, the excitement faded. The saving grace became the perks associated with loyalty programs that reward frequent flyers, hotel guests, and car renters.

For instance, loyalty with a single airline can elevate your status, leading to benefits like priority boarding (ensuring overhead space for your carry-on) or even first-class upgrades. These seemingly small advantages can significantly enhance your travel experience.

Through my extensive travels, I've achieved lifetime loyalty status with both my preferred airline and hotel chain. Speaking of travel, a valuable tip is to avoid checking baggage whenever possible. Learn to pack lightly and efficiently so you can breeze through security with your carry-on luggage.

There's nothing worse than arriving at your destination only to discover a missing suitcase. A final tip: upon reaching your hotel, hang your clothes in the bathroom during your shower. The steam will help remove any wrinkles caused by packing.

Lesson #8: Embracing Discomfort for Growth

The process of writing this book coincided with the passing of my mother and one of my esteemed mentors. These experiences served as a stark reminder of life's brevity and the importance of seizing every opportunity. Nowhere is this principle more applicable than in our careers.

Mark Twain and Confucius are both credited with the famous quote, "Find a job you love, and you will never have to work a day in your life." Similarly, Marsha Sinetar's book title, "Do What You Love, the Money Will Follow," resonates deeply.

Looking back on my career, I wholeheartedly believe in both of these sentiments. I was fortunate to experience immense satisfaction in my work, alongside financial rewards. I firmly believe that everyone has the potential to achieve this.

If you find yourself disengaged, undervalued, or simply going through the motions at work, it's time for a change. The same holds true for personal growth. The absence of discomfort, the absence of those butterflies that accompany challenges, signifies stagnation. If you're not constantly learning, being challenged, and stepping outside your comfort zone, it's time to shake things up.

I understand that change can be daunting. However, no one should have to endure a career filled with dread or disdain. Life is too short to settle for drudgery.

Lesson #9: The Power of Mentorship – Giving and Receiving

If you've gleaned anything from this book, I trust it's the profound impact mentors can have on our professional journeys. The success

I've achieved wouldn't have been possible without the guidance and support of numerous mentors throughout my life. Some offered explicit mentorship, while others unknowingly influenced me through their actions and principles.

Mentorship doesn't require grand gestures or life-altering pronouncements. Sometimes, the most impactful lessons are subtle. For instance, Will Keiper, a mentor from my time at MicroAge, offered a seemingly insignificant yet valuable piece of advice when I transitioned to Compaq Computers. Upon encountering me at a meeting after a year's absence, his first comment was about a tie I'd worn at MicroAge, suggesting I update my wardrobe. Shortly after, I received a package from him containing over 15 ties!

Just as crucial as having mentors is actively seeking opportunities to mentor others. As a CEO, I believe the daily mentorship of associates is paramount. However, there's also merit in identifying individuals with potential who require guidance to refine their skills and advance in their careers. Continuously seek out opportunities to empower and support others on their professional journeys.

Lesson #10: Acting as a Positive Ambassador

Throughout nearly four decades of international travel, I've encountered a perception in some countries that Americans can be loud, wasteful, and self-centered. This is a reputation we don't want to uphold.

An experience at a Chinese airport lounge comes to mind. Four boisterous young American men, fueled by alcohol, were mocking their observations of China. A nearby individual simply leaned over and uttered, "Americans."

Remember, whenever you travel abroad, you represent not only your company but also your country. Your conduct, words, and actions reflect on both entities. Be a positive ambassador by demonstrating respect for local customs and cultures.

Lesson #11: The Generosity of Americans

While I mentioned some negative perceptions of Americans abroad, it's important to highlight a lesser-known fact: Americans are the most charitable people in the world. In 2023 alone, charitable giving in the United States surpassed a staggering $500 billion, with over 75% originating from individuals.

Warren Buffett's "Giving Pledge" exemplifies this philanthropic spirit. He has committed to directing over 99% of his wealth to charitable causes during his lifetime or upon his passing. This remarkable pledge serves as an inspiration to fellow billionaires.

Financial limitations shouldn't deter you from giving back. We all have the power to make a difference. Volunteer your time at a local non-profit, serve on a board, donate financially, or attend fundraising events. Find a cause you're passionate about and dedicate your time or resources to its support. With nearly two million non-profit organizations in the United States, there are countless opportunities to contribute.

Lesson #12: Finding Your Moment of Zen – The Power of Routine

This lesson might sound a bit unconventional, but hear me out. Find an activity you enjoy, something that requires minimal decision-making, allows you to zone out, and provides a sense of accomplishment.

For me, maintaining a lush green lawn has always been a source of pride. I used to spend relaxing weekends mowing our expansive lawn with a riding mower. The rhythmic hum of the engine and the satisfaction of a job well done provided a sense of peace and quiet contemplation.

Discover your own version of this – an activity that allows you to unwind, savor the moment, and perhaps even engage in some introspection. For some, it might be fishing, reading, going for a walk, exercising, or simply a leisurely drive in a cherished car or motorcycle. Carve out time to de-stress and reflect.

Lesson #13: The Art of Active Listening

Here's a fun exercise: track your conversations for a day. Monitor the balance between speaking and truly listening. Active listening goes beyond simply hearing the words being spoken. It requires genuine focus and attentiveness to the speaker's message, absorbing their thoughts and perspectives without formulating your own response prematurely.

Like many others, I readily admit that I haven't always prioritized active listening. We often fall into the trap of viewing conversations as competitions – a battle for the most compelling story, the biggest laugh, or the power to sway the conversation in our favor. This often leads to interruptions and a dominance of our own voices.

The truth is everyone craves being heard and having their ideas acknowledged. Make a conscious effort to practice active listening and observe the positive shift it brings to your interactions. I would argue that the power dynamic favors the listener, not the talker.

Lesson #14: The Power of Positive People

During my college years, I initially planned to major in forestry. My academic advisor, Dr. Robert Larsen, also served as an early mentor. Fresh off a breakup with my girlfriend (who also happened to be a forestry major), I poured my heart out to Dr. Larsen.

While his attempt at sympathy was genuine, his words of wisdom resonated deeply. He shared that friends come and go throughout life, but only a select few become truly close confidantes. Typically, these include a parent and a spouse.

The essence of this lesson lies in the importance of surrounding yourself with positive individuals. I strive to apply this principle when forming my management teams, assembling boards of directors, or participating in committees. We all know those negative people – the ones who see the glass as perpetually half empty. Life is too short to waste time on negativity. Choose to surround yourself with individuals who uplift you, inspire you, and share a positive outlook on the world.

Lesson #15: Prioritizing Family and Well-being

Early on in my career, I set a goal of becoming CEO before the age of 45, granting me eligibility for the Young Presidents' Organization (YPO). I envisioned this organization as a treasure trove of business success secrets, a platform for learning from fellow CEOs.

At the age of 37, my dreams materialized as I was named CEO and President of Artisoft, a publicly traded company based in Tucson, Arizona. One of my first actions was applying for membership in the Arizona chapter of YPO.

My very first YPO meeting, an annual weekend retreat, shattered my preconceptions. Instead of business strategies or market trends, the focus was on personal lives and families. The consensus among these successful leaders was that personal well-being and strong family support were the cornerstones of career success. As long as health, well-being, and family were prioritized, everything else seemed to fall into place. The invaluable lesson I learned from YPO is that neglecting family and self-care ultimately leads to failure. Business challenges can be navigated and resolved with the solid foundation of a supportive family.

These 15 lessons are arguably the most significant factor contributing to my own success and fulfilling career. My wife, Jill, has been my unwavering rock and greatest supporter throughout our 40 years of marriage. She has endured over 20 moves with me, some across the country, others mere streets away. Jill made the selfless decision to prioritize raising our children, Kayci, Matt, and Ross, so I could seize opportunities that came my way.

From YPO and Jill, I learned the most valuable secret to professional success: having a significant other and a family who offer unwavering support and encouragement as you navigate career opportunities.

Vince Lombardi famously stated, "The price of success is hard work, dedication to the job at hand, and the determination that whether we win or lose, we have applied the best of ourselves to the task at hand." This sentiment echoes throughout the lessons shared in this chapter.

While the path to success may not be linear, and there will be setbacks along the way, the unwavering focus on self-improvement, dedication to one's craft, and the pursuit of excellence in all endeavors are the hallmarks of those who achieve their goals.